M000310826

Breaking Down the Barriers

A Guide to Student Services Supervision

Kevin A. Gorman

ROWMAN & LITTLEFIELD EDUCATION
A division of
ROWMAN & LITTLEFIELD PUBLISHERS, INC.
Lanham • New York • Toronto • Plymouth, UK

Published by Rowman & Littlefield Education
A division of Rowman & Littlefield Publishers, Inc.
A wholly owned subsidary of The Rowman & Littlefield Publishing Group, Inc.
4501 Forbes Boulevard, Suite 200, Lanham, Maryland 20706
www.rowman.com

10 Thornbury Road, Plymouth PL6 7PP, United Kingdom

British Library Cataloguing in Publication Information Available

Library of Congress Cataloging-in-Publication Data

Gorman, Kevin A., 1953– .
Breaking down the barriers : a guide to student services supervision / Kevin Gorman. pages.
p. cm.
Includes index.
ISBN 978-1-61048-937-9 (cloth : alk. paper) — ISBN 978-1-4758-0085-2 (pbk. : alk. paper) — ISBN 978-1-4758-0091-3 (electronic)
1. School supervision—United States—Handbooks, manuals, etc. 2. School management and organization—United States—Handbooks, manuals, etc. 3. Students—Services for—United States. I. Title.
LB2806.4.G67 2012
371.2'03—dc23
2012051450

™
The paper used in this publication meets the minimum requirements of American National Standard for Information Sciences Permanence of Paper for Printed Library Materials, ANSI/NISO Z39.48-1992.

Printed in the United States of America

A community that excludes even one of its members is no community at all. —Dan Wilkins

Contents

Foreword

Understanding, experience, and commitment to educational leadership are what Kevin Gorman brings to the writing of this book. I first met Kevin more than thirty years ago when I was a young teacher of children with autism. He provided me with support and coaching in the design of a behavior plan for a young, institutionalized student with autism. Since that time, our career paths have paralleled and intertwined.

I have known Kevin as a special education supervisor, a high school principal, and a director of student services. In every position, Kevin has brought advocacy and a steadfast commitment to educating diverse learners and providing the resources and training needed by teachers to fulfill this obligation. Whether talking with parents, teachers, or other administrators, the impact on student learning and well-being guides the discussion.

This book is a resource for those interested in becoming supervisors and directors of services for diverse learners (special education, English-language learners, gifted) and practicing school administrators who may have acquired responsibilities to oversee specific programs designed to support diverse learners. Throughout the book Kevin's philosophy of educating each student to the maximum shines through.

The importance of knowing each student, communicating and working with parents, and supporting teachers with resources and professional development are emphasized. As professional educators and administrators, Kevin takes us beyond the need to remain current in our knowledge of legal requirements and research to translating the information into action and practice to meet the needs of students. He brings the voice of reason in the design of educational programs, understanding of what is working, and use of specialists to support the design, implementation, and monitoring of student educational services.

The process for getting to highly effective educational services is also provided through the use of collaborative workgroups with school, parent, and community representatives and that spirit that says go out and seek the information and expertise needed to understand and solve educational challenges. As Kevin so eloquently states, *"It is the director's ethical obligation to ensure that all children are getting the necessary services that will make them successful during the school year and for life."*

Educational leadership comes in many different forms in the complex world of education as we know it today. Kevin's sharing of his insight based on his experience as an educational leader is a gift to both current and future administrators in the areas of student services.

Sue Zake, Ph.D.
Director of the Office for Exceptional Children
Ohio Department of Education

Preface

Student intervention has become increasingly important in K–12 education in the last few years. The Individual Disabilities Education Act (IDEA) in 2004 laid out guidelines for schools to follow in special education assessment and placement. With Race to the Top and the Common Core and districts now able to opt out of No Child Left Behind, the rules and the game have all changed for public schools. Schools are now held accountable not just as a system, but individual principals and teachers are also a part of the accountability and rating scale that is published locally, and they are evaluated on the percentage of students demonstrating a year's growth in progress.

This has created a sense of urgency and is a catalyst for change in public education. Schools are now looking at the service providers within the school, universal screeners, and student outcomes in a different light. Children who have been a part of a pull-out special needs program now are being included more so that access to rich content information is not lost on the part of the student and so that the student can score higher on the required annual state assessments.

This book is about intervention for *all* children. Chapter 1 describes an overview of intervention and response to intervention. The rest of the book examines different areas of exceptionality from autism to children with emotional disturbance and cognitive delays, due process and individualized educational plans (IEPs) and 504 plans. Parent relationships are emphasized along with what programming should entail so that *all* students demonstrate growth and how teachers can utilize targeted research-based strategies to ensure that these children are successful. This book is different in that it separates the theory from the "how to," yet that "how to" is based upon the theory that is shared in each chapter. Few books break down the identifica-

tion of each disability and give evidence-based strategies that will assist
student programming and student success.

Relationship building with difficult teachers and parents will be embedded throughout each chapter.

This book is a necessary vehicle to train special education supervisors and
would-be directors in how to develop a plan that is strategic for the district,
yet always student centered. Too often decisions are based solely upon fi-
nances, and supervisors just follow the law with nothing extra. The law was
written as a mere minimum of services and not what necessarily each and
every student might need to be successful.

This text was developed to train new supervisory professionals in the
field, as well as thinking out of the box to suggest services rather than just the
minimum requirements. Many of the veterans who grew up with the law are
now retiring and moving on to other ventures. This book provides the new
supervisor details of experience and evidence-based suggestions on how to
put the student first and how to develop relationships with parents and teachers.

This book can be read by looking at single chapters of interest or in its
entirety. Hopefully, it will serve as a desktop reference for the new genera-
tion of special education administrators in the field of education.

Introduction

Special education continues to progress in accountability for all professionals. This accountability can present difficult situations for all administrators from veterans to those that are new to the supervisory experience. Children with special needs present with sometimes difficult scenarios to problem solve educational solutions and meet the individual needs of the child.

Most of the problems or issues that develop in individualized educational plan (IEP) meetings are adult issues and only indirectly involved the child. Schools sometimes do not have the financial means or do not think creatively enough to determine a way to meet the needs of a child. Sometimes parents have unrealistic viewpoints of where and what their child should be accomplishing in school. In both situations, the parents just want what is best for their child, and educators need to realize how they would advocate if this was their child with these needs.

This book is a guide to student services looking at all aspects of student needs. Each chapter presents the theory behind the practice that is suggested in the second half of each chapter. The reader can just read the research or can just read the suggested proactive practice, having confidence that it is all evidence based.

At the end of each chapter are case scenarios of possible problems or issues that could develop in that particular area of need. The answers to the case studies are not given, but the hope is that the research will assist the reader in determining appropriate student-centered solutions to the problem(s) presented. In student services, there is no right or wrong response to student concerns, as long as the supervisor determines, with the assistance of a team, how to ensure that the student in question is always the focus of all educational recommendations and that he or she can reach his or her fullest potential in education as well as in life.

Chapter One

Intervention

THEORY

Student achievement outcome data is being published nationally, as is the rating or grading of the teachers and administrators who have worked with these students for the past school year. Against this instructional backdrop, teachers are trying to do business differently than in the past because these instructors also literally want to make the grade. Tiered levels of intervention are being utilized to assist students who may be struggling academically or behaviorally. Intervention is now being utilized for *all* students and not just those who are failing quarterly content classes.

Children come into school with different levels of learning readiness. Schools finally are addressing those different levels of academic preparedness by intervening early and developing prevention activities, rather than waiting for students to be unsuccessful throughout the first few years of school (Fuchs, Fuchs, & Compton, 2010).

Prior to the No Child Left Behind Act (2001), children had to fail to receive assistance. Subjective quarterly teacher grades were utilized to determine failure, learning difficulties, or outcomes. The response to these difficulties was an assessment, and placement in some formal type of intervention called either a Title Program or Special Education. These programs were considered a place not a service.

If a child could be identified with a problem, he or she then could be placed in another room to receive assistance. Though this placement was intended to remediate, it appeared more to keep the child current with the typical classroom teacher work load and did little to assist the child with the learning issues that he or she had. The issue exacerbated itself even more because the child was being pulled out of the classroom for remediation, was

1

missing more and more content, and was falling further and further behind. It became almost a self-fulfilling prophecy.

Response to Intervention (RTI) has been present in elementary schools for years, although it may have been called different things. It looks different in every school. School personnel must be committed to working together to make a systemic change in how they intervene and progress monitor each individual student.

The change that has to occur is that all curricular decisions must be made on student data (Ehren, 2010). Most schools are using formative assessment as one means to evaluate the success or failure of a content lesson.

Data must be gathered from different data points that are normed nationally so that student literacy can be measured, and intervention and/or enrichment activities can be developed to impact student learning and performance.

These activities or instructional strategies can and should be targeted in meeting the individual needs of the students (Duffy, 2007). Once the learning targets have been established, then the schedule has to be considered, so that children who are struggling get a double or triple dose of instruction in their deficit areas. Ongoing use of universal screeners can be used to determine deficit or gaps in the learning sequence.

Universal screeners are assessments that have been normed nationally and can measure individual progress and progress deficits (Canter, Klotz, & Cowan, 2008). A strategy used within the classroom needs to be evidence-based if a child is going to be successful. Too often re-teaching did not involve evidence-based strategies that have been proven to be effective in remediation. Instructors would just re-teach the same material or same skill in the same way that they had previously taught the material and would get frustrated at the negative outcome of that teaching strategy.

RTI is a shift in thinking and instruction. Teachers now can determine what they can do to reinforce a concept, rather than waiting for a student to fail before intervening (Burns, 2008).

INTEGRATING THEORY INTO PRACTICE

At the beginning of every school year, students need to be screened utilizing a universal nationally normed instrument in the areas of reading, writing, and mathematics. Children who score in the lower ten to twenty-five percent based upon this screener need intervention. Reading and math specialists can assist in this endeavor.

Reading and math intervention specialists may or may not have any evidence-based strategies to intervene. It is imperative that the school leaders find the instructional strategies that the instructor needs to remediate before the children are screened for intervention.

Children who are new and move into the district should also be screened during the registration process. This ensures that if intervention is needed, the new students will get assistance immediately upon their enrollment. Transient students with literacy issues sometimes were not discovered and went undiagnosed for months at a time because universal screeners were not used during their enrollment process.

Progress monitoring should occur district-wide on a regularly scheduled date throughout the school year to ensure progress is being made using the research-based strategies. Most book sellers now are using research as a means to sell their materials, making suitable teaching tools more widely accessible to school districts. Having an administrator look at what is available and then having a board of education adopt those materials will ensure that students are being taught properly and that literacy deficits in both reading and math are being addressed and corrected. This could almost be used as script teaching to ensure everyone is being exposed to the same evidence-based strategy.

The systemic change that must occur in every building has to be looking at special education differently. Special education can no longer be a place where children are evaluated and left for lost for the rest of their school career. This not only deprives students who are being pulled from content information but also creates a learned helplessness among the students who are in special education.

As students transition out of high school, this helplessness and lack of content knowledge creates situations in which students cannot or do not get accepted to any kind of postsecondary training, or if they are successful entering, tend to fail or drop out because they have never learned how to advocate for themselves.

The other change has to occur with the education of parents. Parents are used to evaluating the success of their intervention specialist by the grades their child earns in his or her classes. The intervention specialist trying to keep a child current with his or her content area teacher does not have time to remediate but rather spends sessions helping with homework and organization.

If true intervention is to take place, then parents are going to have to get on the train to intervention, realizing that much of the homework assigned at school will come home with their child to complete at home. This is a radical shift in parent and district philosophy in most schools throughout the country, but a critical improvement that frees the intervention teacher to address skill deficits not work completion.

This type of intervention is essential if schools want to increase the literacy rate in their classrooms. With local media publications grading teachers and administrators there is now a sense of urgency among schools and the instructors for this change process. Educational leaders need to use this catalyst to make the changes necessary so that *all* children can learn and be literate.

CASE STUDIES

- A student qualifies for a multifactored evaluation after numerous interventions. At the evaluation planning meeting, the parent requests intervention during the time it takes to complete the evaluation. The parent is denied by the team. What probably is going to be the parent's next reaction or action?
- A student continues to struggle in certain concepts and is placed in a small group pull-out tier-two intervention. The child is not progress monitored and remains for the rest of the school semester in tier-two intervention. What should the parent be asking the team?
- As a supervisor in special education a teacher requests paraprofessional support to work in his or her classroom for tier-one interventions. Is this appropriate, and what suggestions can the supervisor give to the classroom teacher?

REFERENCES

Burns, M. (2008). Response to Intervention at the Secondary Level. *Principal Leadership* Vol. 8, No. 7: 12–15.

Canter, A., Klotz, M. B., & Cowan, K. (2008). Response to Intervention: The Future for Secondary Schools. *Principal Leadership*, Vol. 8, No. 6: 12–15.

Duffy, H. (2007). *Meeting the Needs of Significantly Struggling Learners in High School*. National High School Center. Retrieved December 17, 2012, from http://www.betterhighschools.org/docs/NHSC_RTIBrief_08-02-07.pdf.

Ehren, B. (2010). Use of RTI with Older Students Is Growing. *Reading Today*, Vol. 28, No. 1: 10.

Fuchs, L., Fuchs, D., & Compton, D. (2010). Rethinking Response to Intervention at Middle and High School. *School Psychology Review*, Vol. 39, No. 1: 22–28.

POINTS TO REMEMBER

- All school systems must implement a universal screener to assess who is falling behind grade level. New enrollees should also be screened so that they can be placed in the appropriate section or class.
- Benchmarking is a means of collecting a baseline on a student. Progress monitoring should be completed at set intervals throughout the school year.
- Special education needs to be a service not a place where children receive intervention.

Chapter Two

The Laws

THEORY

The spirit of the Individuals with Disabilities Education Act (IDEA) of 2004 is interpreted a bit differently in each state. The initial purpose of the act was to provide a free and appropriate public education (FAPE) for all children identified as having a disability, as well as to ensure that the rights of children with disabilities and the parents of these children are protected under the law.

As each state implements this law, the effectiveness varies from state to state depending on the individual interpretation. The purpose of the law was to improve academic achievement and performance of children with disabilities on measurable state assessments as compared to children without disabilities. IDEA intends children to be included more in the general education curriculum, as well as to improve transitions at natural times in the child's school career (Blackorby, 2010).

The act also intends for children identified with disabilities, including minority children, to be placed in the least restrictive environment (LRE). Having children in the LRE ensures that children with emotional disturbances and specific learning disabilities will not drop out of school as readily as those that are placed in separate facilities or are otherwise isolated from typical peers.

IDEA also addresses literacy concerns and reading instruction for children with disabilities, ensuring that schools utilize evidence-based strategies in a systematic approach in teaching these skills. The act also provides guidelines to ensure parents are involved every step of the way from intervention to identification to placement and treatment of the student in his or her deficit areas. Resolution to disagreements is also a part of this act.

Another law that sometimes gets confused with IDEA is Section 504 of the Rehabilitation Act of 1973. Section 504 provides protection against discrimination for individuals with disabilities. Section 504 protects students in school if they are not already eligible under the eligibility requirements of IDEA.

A student is eligible and entitled to a Section 504 accommodation plan if an evaluation demonstrates that the individual has a mental or physical impairment that substantially limits one or more major life activities. Learning could be one of those activities. The result can be an accommodation plan and usually begins with the Response to Intervention (RTI) team.

When a student has not responded positively to tiered interventions, the team may consider the top tier or one-to-one intervention to assist the student in being successful. The team usually consists of an administrator, a counselor, a classroom teacher, and the parent. Secondary students should also be a part of the team.

Many schools are leery about implementing any or many 504 plans because they are not federally or state funded. All costs incurred are the responsibility of the school district budget as opposed to individualized educational plans (IEPs) and special education plans that are often funded. The other concern of many schools hesitant to develop a 504 plan is that this is a general education initiative, and the case manager is the classroom teacher. The concern arises if the general education teacher has a large caseload, then the 504 accommodations will be missed or forgotten. However, it is a legal document and no different than an IEP in terms of fulfilling the accommodations listed on the plan.

If a 504 plan is not followed, and a parent wants to pursue further action, it goes to court. If an IEP is not followed it goes to due process after mediation. For a 504, the plan accommodations may stop while the case is being heard, whereas on an IEP the student "stays put" until some type of resolution is reached by all parties.

Most 504 plans occur at the secondary level, formalizing the accommodations that are just strong teaching practices. Accommodations are different than modifications. A modification substantially changes the general education curriculum, whereas an accommodation provides opportunities for an adjustment in the presentation of the material or assessment but does not change the content in any way. An IEP can and usually does have both accommodations and modifications, whereas a 504 plan only has accommodations.

INTEGRATING THEORY INTO PRACTICE

Many times when a student does not qualify for an IEP, the team determines that the student still needs some type of assistance. This assistance should be in the form of a tiered intervention; however, sometimes teams are tempted to offer a 504 plan as a consolation prize for not receiving the IEP. There should always be a documented legitimate reason and rationale for placing anyone on a 504 plan.

During evaluation and development, 504 meetings should include a team. A 504 plan is usually written for a year, but if problems arise, it should be a work in progress because meetings should be scheduled to address the problem. The team should include a district representative, guidance counselors, and the student and classroom teachers. All teachers should attend so that an accommodation that cannot work in his or her classroom can be amended so that the student can be successful and the teacher has input in the development of the plan.

A 504 plan should also include the student in the planning meeting. Many times adults will develop ideas, thinking that the student will be successful by implementing the accommodation, and the student may not want any part of it. The student needs to be asked if he or she will participate in whatever the accommodation being suggested for the plan development entails. Very often students, especially secondary students, have their own ideas of what will work or not work for them in the 504 plan. Schools and staff members can be set up unintentionally if the student is not an active part of the team.

Students need to be involved in both the IEP process and the 504 process, especially for adolescents. As adults develop interventions to be written into an IEP or 504 plan the adolescent must be a part of the process. Sometimes adults come up with plans that the teen has no intention of complying with, and the plan has no way of working. It is essential that the IEP and 504 plans have student buy-in so that any plan written can be successful.

All members of the team should receive a copy of the 504 plan and the IEP once all signatures have been secured. Teachers need to be knowledgeable regarding the demands of the plan. A file of the plan should be kept in the school, as well as the district office.

A 504 plan and an IEP should only be developed when the concern is affecting academic progress. If things are happening only in the home, then other outside resources should be suggested. If a school official recommends any type of service, the school district is responsible financially for providing that service.

If the team feels the family needs help sometimes, saying something like, "If he were my son I would probably look at this program or service," this takes the recommendation out of the picture. However, there is a very fine line between a suggestion and a recommendation, and all it takes is for the parent to seek legal advice for it really to become an issue.

The law requires a team approach in IEP development and 504 development because it works. As professionals, parents, and students gather to brainstorm a problem, different solutions develop, a successful measurable plan is developed, and in the end the student is the winner.

CASE STUDIES

- The parent expresses concern at the meeting that the child is spending an inordinate amount of time on homework and therefore needs an IEP to facilitate this issue. The team offers to shorten the amount of work given every night to accommodate this problem. Is a 504 plan necessary to accomplish this goal?
- A guidance counselor develops a 504 plan with the parent but does not invite the student or the teachers to the conference. After the conference the counselor gathers the signatures of the teachers and the student and then copies the plan and distributes the 504 to all team members. The plan is much more complicated than the teachers can implement. As a supervisor you receive an email from the parent claiming the plan is not being followed. What is your responsibility because it is a regular education initiative?
- An IEP conference is convened; however, the parent does not sign the IEP because he or she wants to consult with an outside advocate before committing to the goals and objectives. The current IEP is expiring before the team can reconvene. Does the intervention specialist implement the old expired IEP or the new unsigned IEP?
- A student is being removed from an IEP and special education services. The parent requests a 504 plan in place of the IEP. The team denies the request. Is this appropriate or not for this student?

REFERENCES

Blackorby, J. (2010). "Patterns in the Identification of and Outcomes for Children and Youth with Disabilities," NCEE 2010-4006 (National Center for Education evaluation and Regional Assistance, Institute of Education Sciences, US Department of Education).

Bradley, M. C., et al. (2011). *IDEA National Assessment Implementation Study* (NCEE 2011–4027). Washington, DC: National Center for Educational and Regional Assistance, Institute of Education Sciences, U.S. Department of Education.

U.S. Department of Education, Office of Civil Rights, Denver, Colorado. (2007). http://www.ed.gov/about/offices/list/ocr/docs/disabharassltr.html. Retrieved 9/15/2012.

U.S. Department of Education, Office of Special Education and Rehabilitative Services, Office of Special Education Programs. (2009). *28th Annual Report to Congress on the Implementation of the Individuals with Disabilities Education Act*, 2006, vol. 1, Washington, DC: Author.

POINTS TO REMEMBER

- The Individuals with Disabilities Education Act was authorized to provide a free and appropriate public education for all children.
- The law also addresses intervention as something that utilizes evidence-based strategies that will make a significant positive difference in the life of a child.
- Section 504 of the Rehabilitation Act of 1973 describes the section that a person with a medical impairment cannot be discriminated against. This is the rationale for a 504 plan.
- Prior to a multifactored evaluation, a school team must intervene, look at the data, and respond appropriately to that data and make decisions. This is called Response to Intervention.
- Individualized education plans can generate federal funding; however, 504 plans are a general education initiative and the cost is picked up by the school district.

Chapter Three

Autism

THEORY

The Individuals with Disabilities Education Act (IDEA) of 2004 is riddled with references about the need to utilize research-supported treatments and practices when working with children. Research is essential, but so is common sense, especially when working with individuals on the autism spectrum. The implementation of research-supported interventions and evidence-based treatment procedures also must take into consideration the family's preferences, the instructor's professional judgment, and the accuracy of the implementation process and procedures (Autism Speaks, 2011) before ever implementing a practice.

Autism is a medical diagnosis, though there are no clear-cut medical tests that can make that determination. It is a spectrum disorder indicating that the child's impairment can vary from intensive to mild or moderate in how it presents itself behaviorally. Children on the spectrum may have characteristics of social deficits, behavior issues, communication delays, sensory or motor deficits, or a lack of emotional awareness. The cause of autism is unknown, but the researchers have ascertained that there are obviously some brain abnormalities. In June 2012, many of the frozen brains that displayed these abnormalities were lost due to a freezer malfunction, so the medical research has been set back drastically.

In the recent past in K–12, education supervisors and directors put children into categories or pockets of similar behaviors or learning styles once the child had been identified as having a disability. The child would be placed into an established classroom that matched, to some degree, the outcome of the child's evaluation and the availability of classroom space based upon state recommendations for enrollment for that particular disability label. Autism, if treated appropriately, does not have a one-size-fits-all treatment option.

If a teacher sees one child that has autism, the teacher has seen one child that has autism. Every child on the spectrum presents differently with different needs. All children are unique, and as more information is learned about children on the spectrum and their learning needs, supervisors and directors can generalize this philosophy to their everyday practice. Treating children as individuals with different needs, rather than as numbers, or attempting to place a child in services that are already established within a district instead of thinking out of the box for that specific child's needs, is a travesty and truly does not represent the intended spirit of IDEA. Remember special education should be a service not a place.

When working with individuals with autism or any type of atypical behavior, the professional must observe the child. The antecedent for the behavior (as to what triggered the response from the child) must be examined, as well as the behavior that was displayed following the outburst. Consequences and how the child responds to those consequences are essential in treating and maintaining or extinguishing that behavior. Consistency is key when working with children on the spectrum.

Many children on the autism spectrum have difficulty interpreting and comprehending verbal language and may depend upon prompts to understand the request or statement. Prompts can be physical (hand over hand), visual, gestural, and even verbal. If a student on the spectrum is presented with conversation, the child will lose focus. Any verbalization needs to be short and to the point and is often most effective when paired with visuals.

There is a model called the Ziggurat Model for determining the needs of a child on the spectrum (Ziggurat Group). A team including the parent sits in a meeting and determines the skills that are needed to be taught, the demands of the task being asked of the student, the types of supports the student may need, the reinforcers that motivate the student, and any sensory or biological needs the student may present within school (Ziggurat Model). Looking at such a structure can make a positive difference in the life of a student on the spectrum.

Examining sensory needs is critical in how they affect learning. A child with sensory needs feels like he or she has an itch that cannot be scratched. That type of distraction limits or prohibits task completion. An occupational therapist is a good evaluator as to what needs the child must have before he or she begins schoolwork. Those needs can be met using a sensory diet or activities designed to meet that need like scratching an itch.

A child on the spectrum thrives on structure and predictability to be successful. He or she must know what the task is, when he or she will be done with the task, and that the reinforcer that will reward them for task completion. Utilizing a board-certified behavior analyst is the best way to ensure the activities and the reinforcers are all evidence-based and are followed with fidelity.

Other specialists needed to provide a strong program include a speech pathologist, who can assist with augmentative technology to assist with communication and social skills, and an adaptive physical education instructor, who can assist with developmentally appropriate motor skills prior to participating in any physical games or activities. All of these specialists would need to be written into the individualized educational plan (IEP) of the student, only if appropriate to the individualized needs of that student.

The National Autism Center (2009) completed a standards-based project that identified key research-based interventions that proved successful for children and adolescents on the autism spectrum. From this report, eleven established treatments were suggested with twenty-two emerging treatments that do not yet have the evidence or the proven effectiveness over time to be considered as working established treatments. This chapter will focus on the eleven established interventions.

The different interventions need to be developed by a specialist in behavior observing, collecting data on each individual child, and should not be treated lightly by an instructor. The antecedent package or treatment has been effective with children from ages three to eighteen years. It involves choice, behavior chain interruption, controlling stimuli, and errorless learning. A board-certified behavior analyst would be the specialist to instruct and implement these eleven researched interventions.

The behavioral intervention is based upon observation and collecting data. The actual evaluation needs to involve what happened prior to the behavior (antecedent), and what the outcome after the behavior (consequences) is. The key to this program is changing consequences based upon the individual need of the child and attempting to improve performance based upon the consequences implemented. This intervention obviously works throughout a student's school life, as everyone reacts to consequences.

The third evidence-based intervention involves a complete behavior childhood program. This delivery model utilizes applied behavior analysis (ABA) that targets the characteristics of autism spectrum disorders. A board-certified behavior analyst can only develop the program, and only a trained behaviorist can implement the intervention. The ages that the research suggests are until the age of about nine years old. ABA includes behaviors in the communication arena, cognitive skills, interpersonal skills, motor skills, play skills, and problem behaviors that are a part of the disorder. Treatment is, on an average, an intensive twenty-five hours per week at home and at school.

Joint attention intervention involves two individuals focusing simultaneously on an object, on each other, or on a joint activity. The instructor observes the student's eye gaze or how a child responds to a prompt or an activity that they both are participating in together. The activity needs to be reinforcing for the student, and prompting is essential. This intervention works for children up to five years of age and has demonstrated that communication and interpersonal skills have shown improvement if done correctly and with fidelity.

Modeling is another intervention that has shown effectiveness between the ages of three and eighteen years. Modeling may occur through the use of video or live modeling using a demonstration of a target behavior in front of a child who is on the autism spectrum. Video modeling has proven to be cost effective because multiple students can utilize the program throughout a school day, and it allows the instructor to stop the disc at certain points to repeat characteristics that need to be emphasized to the student.

Naturalistic teaching permits the instructor to implement direct and natural consequences that relate directly to the target behavior. It allows children to generalize specific skills in different settings and scenarios. Different materials and settings should be utilized when teaching to enhance the generalization of the programming. Following a student's interest is a good technique to motivate the child, as well as observing his or her behavior of interaction with the motivator. This technique has worked with children up to the age of nine who are on the autism spectrum.

Peer training is another intervention that may motivate children on the spectrum. Peers should be trained, socially skilled, able to imitate a model, and take direction from an instructor. Having a peer model allows children to play together and interact both on a verbal and nonverbal basis. Typical peers may be very motivating for some children on the spectrum up to the age of fourteen. Peer modeling may decrease inappropriate self-stimulation and repetitive behaviors that distract from meaningful interaction with others.

Pivotal response treatment has shown to be effective for children up to the age of nine. This intervention targets self-motivation by providing choices, self-initiation by following a visual schedule, and self-management by having the student chart his or her own behavior and respond to many different cues or prompts to elicit a specific behavior.

Schedules are an intervention unto themselves. They provide the opportunity for a child to be able to predict what will happen next. Predictability is a comfort to many people on the spectrum. Schedules may include pictures or photographs of the activity. Students can move the picture or sentence from the schedule, prompting a feeling of control over the child's day. Reinforcement should be included in the schedule as an additional motivation. This treatment is wonderful for children up to the age of eighteen. Use of schedules improves self-regulation as well as academic and interpersonal skills by providing that predictability to the child's daily routine.

Story-based intervention allows for a written type of social story that predicts the outcome of the instructor-selected activity. The story includes the who, what, where, when, why, and how questions usually written in the first person point of view to assist the student in being successful. The story is usually read prior to the child engaging in the desired activity. This technique has worked up to the age of fourteen years of age. The technique assists with communication, interpersonal skills, understanding emotions, self-regulation, and problem behavior.

Though there are eleven different researched treatments that have been proven successful, it is still essential for the instructor to utilize the appropriate specialists for observation, training, and implementation; use professional judgment; and involve the parent in all decision making prior to any implementation. Parent involvement is essential to promote consistency between treatment at home and treatment in school. All observations, program development, and program data should be in writing and shared and must be signed off by the family prior to implementation.

INTEGRATING THEORY INTO PRACTICE

Children on the autism spectrum truly are unique individuals. Working with children on the spectrum allows the special education supervisor or coordinator to initiate the fidelity and the spirit of IDEA by looking at each child as an individual and developing a program around the child's needs rather than placing the child in a specific program that may be already developed within the school system. As was stated, *once you have seen one person with autism you have seen one person with autism.*

It is essential that all children on the autism spectrum utilize, as early as possible, research-based interventions that have been proven to be successful over time. All treatment decisions need to be developed as a team based upon data, research, and specialists. All the child's service providers, including the parents, need to be part of all decisions made by the school. Professional judgment should play an important role in treatment decisions. A one-size-fits-all treatment plan does not work with children on the spectrum.

The values and preferences of the family must be taken into consideration when working with children. Some treatments may be contrary to the belief system of the family, or the individual student may indicate that he or she wants no part in the plan to be implemented. If a specific treatment was implemented incorrectly in the past, then the effects of that treatment may adversely affect the individual or the individual's behavior. The fidelity of treatment must be followed to ensure a successful intervention.

Many times, instructors feel like they know what should be done as they have worked with the child with autism for a while and feel threatened when a specialist comes in and questions or makes suggestions to the treatment plan. It is the responsibility of the supervisor to ensure that the expert is listened to and the suggestions to the team are followed and not sabotaged by the classroom instructor because of an ego issue. Many times in self-contained classroom situations, the supervisor may or may not be aware of what is happening behind closed doors. This means that observations, written documentation, and data collection through multiple sources are essential for the determination of the fidelity of the program being implemented.

The primary factor in finding success with a child on the spectrum is implementing programs that are evidence based to show success and are supervised by a behavioral specialist that has the education, the extended practice, and the board certification to facilitate appropriate programming for the student.

CASE STUDIES

- As a supervisor you contract with a board-certified behavior analyst to assist as a consultant in an autism classroom. The behavior consultant contacts you to give you a list of suggestions and recommendations made to the instructor. As a supervisor you observe the classroom and the instructor explains that most of the recommendations are inappropriate to be used in this particular classroom. How do you sort through the concerns, support the instructor, and ensure that the student's needs are being met appropriately? Does the teacher know more about behavior than the specialist?
- You receive a call from your autism classroom teacher explaining that the typical inclusive classroom teacher keeps sending worksheets to be completed by the student in the autism room, which compromises the work he or she is trying to implement in his or her classroom. The typical classroom instructor will not allow the student to return if he or she is not current with the topic during the inclusive setting because the student's behavior is disrupting the class when he or she does not comprehend what is happening in the typical classroom. What is your response?
- The paraprofessional working with the autism instructor has been writing in the student's daily communication log with the parent. When the paraprofessional takes the student to his or her car the parent asks what is happening in the classroom because she or he is not hearing from the instructor. The paraprofessional tells the parent that the instructor does not appear very competent to him or her. As a supervisor you receive a call from the parent. What is your next move?

REFERENCES

Attwood, T. (2007). *The Complete Guide to Asperger's Syndrome*. Philadelphia: Jessica Kingsley Publishers.
Autism Speaks. www.autismspeaks.org. Retrieved August 5, 2012.

Lee, S., Odom, S. L., & Loftin, R. (2007). Social Engagement with Peers and Stereotypic Behavior of Children with Autism. *Journal of Positive Behavior Interventions*, Vol. 9: 67–79.

Lord, C., & McGee, J. P. National Research Council, Committee on Educational Interventions for Children with Autism. (2001). *Educating Children with Autism.* Washington, DC: National Academy Press.

National Autism Center. (2009). *Evidence-Based Practice and Autism in the Schools*. Retrieved June 25, 2012, from nationalautismcenter.org.

O'Brien, M., & Dagget, J. (2006). *Beyond the Autism Diagnosis: A Professional's Guide to Helping Families*. Baltimore, MD: Brooks Publishing.

Pelios, L. V., MacDuff, G. S., & Axelrod, S. (2003). The Effects of a Treatment Package in Establishing Independent Academic Work Skills in Children with Autism. *Education and Treatment of Children*, Vol. 26, No. 1: 1–21.

POINTS TO REMEMBER

- If you have seen one child with autism you have seen one child with autism. Children who have autism present very differently from one another.
- Children with autism do respond better with visuals and evidence-based treatment programs.
- Applied behavior analysis is a systematic treatment program, which is one of the only programs that has evidence that it does make a positive difference in children with autism.
- Children with autism perform better with appropriate peer models. Video modeling also has proven to make a positive difference with children with autism.
- Sensory input can assist a student in self-regulation.
- Autism is a medical diagnosis. Just because a student has the label of having autism does not mean that he or she immediately needs an IEP or 504 plan. Those should only be implemented if the autism is having an adverse effect of either academics or social interaction with peers.

Chapter Four

Gifted and Talented

THEORY

Response to Intervention (RTI) is a vehicle that needs to be considered when working with gifted children. The three tiers should be divided just as they are for at-risk children. Gifted children are at risk for lower achievement if their instruction is not altered to meet their individual needs. Using the RTI model, tier one could be handled within the classroom through differentiation. Differentiation is not busy work, but rather challenges students at the actual levels of the student's achievement. Tier two might involve utilizing a gifted intervention instructor to compact the curriculum, developing enrichment activities, or even accelerating in certain subject area(s) (Hughs & Rollins, 2009). Tier three involves acceleration or pull out gifted group activities based upon a pre-established criterion. Inclusion rather than exclusion has to be the philosophy of RTI and gifted education.

Interventions in gifted education must be handled with fidelity. The decisions made for instruction must be data driven, and best practice must be considered in all instruction (Coleman & Gallagher, 1995). Children who are identified as gifted have the right to continue to make annual progress, no matter at what high achievement level they are beginning each school year.

Continuity of instruction must also be considered when working with the gifted-and-talented population. Many elementary programs may use a pull-out language arts program in serving children that are identified, and then at the junior high, acceleration might be the only means to service adolescents. The high school may offer a mix of honors or advanced placement (AP) classes. Unfortunately there is no continuity between the programming, and they are each separate entities unto themselves. Gifted education must develop in each school system some type of framework that supports a coherent program between grade levels and school buildings (Brown & Abernethy, 2009).

If gifted education is going to continue as an entity, the field must adopt the principles of the general core curriculum while keeping the "exceptionality concept" of instructional techniques that best represents the gifted population needs (VanTassel-Baska, 2003). District policy and guidelines must be considered and rewritten to ensure continuity between programs, and grade levels exists so that a consistent approach to gifted education is inherent in the approach to instruction.

Special education has the Individuals with Disabilities Education Act (IDEA) to guide the approach and philosophy of serving children with special needs. Districts adopt the federal law and the policies that are dictated by both state and federal laws. Gifted education does not have that same luxury to base its policy development and instructional guidelines on, yet children who are identified as gifted also have special needs that must be addressed. Gifted education is not a privilege. It is a right.

Many states require gifted identification but then do not require mandated programming for these identified students. This is truly ironic. It devalues the needs of a student with special needs. Without appropriate instruction, this population—gifted and talented—hits a glass ceiling in terms of academic growth that forces their achievement level back to the mean (Brown & Abernethy, 2009). There is so much media talk regarding global educational competition with other countries, and yet educationally the states suppress those students that could compete on the global market by not offering standardized policy and programs for gifted education.

INTEGRATING THEORY INTO PRACTICE

Whether a child is in preschool or high school, gifted children need the rigor increased along with integrating critical thinking skills. One of the issues with the core curriculum is that most teachers will teach to the test and not initially go beyond the Common Core. This can be attributed to the instructor's learning curve and also worrying about student test scores and how it reflects his or her teaching skill set on the published district report card at the end of the year.

A gifted student's educational progress relies heavily on formal learning in the classroom, going beyond the Common Core curriculum. Instructors worry mostly about catching the at-risk student up so that his or her test scores show a year's growth in achievement. However, the issue of test score growth is also magnified by not addressing the needs of the children who are gifted and talented. The classroom instructor is putting the gifted children at risk by not addressing their needs. These students will not show growth, and the lack of appropriate instruction could create stagnation or a turn-off for these same students.

Decision making infused within critical thinking will help the gifted student internalize guided questions so that through meta-cognition the students can think about their decision-making process using their critical thinking skills. Unfortunately, although this sounds like a great idea, having a teacher differentiate enough to allow this to happen can be difficult to say the least.

As a gifted supervisor the entire gifted program needs to be evaluated and possibly restructured or changed to meet the needs of these students, especially if they are within the typical classroom. A gifted intervention specialist can mirror co-teaching, as it is practiced in special education, working with students in clustered groups to ensure they are being challenged. This allows the formal learning for children that is necessary for all students but also challenges the gifted student's scholastic rigor. The rigor will stimulate the child intellectually and enhance their academic growth.

If a pull-out program is used for gifted instruction, then the gifted intervention specialist should consult weekly with the typical classroom teacher to ensure he or she is following the same scope and sequence of that child's general classroom. This is important for two reasons. When children return to the typical classroom they should not feel lost or unsure as to what they might have missed while participating in the pull-out program. This could cause insecurity and a negative reaction for students. It also gives some serious direction to the gifted intervention specialist as to the standards that they too should be following; the specialist should be responsible for ensuring the children are having their academic needs met while still providing the extra rigor and challenges needed.

If acceleration is used for subject area classes or a whole grade level, then some type of evidence-based protocol should be used as a guideline or vehicle to make that decision. Most of these protocols look at the entire child. Intellectual functioning should only be one facet that is considered for acceleration. Grade levels of siblings, a child's developmental factors, social skill sets of the child, and finally student attitude and support should be a part of any protocol used and a part of the team decision-making process.

Parent education should be a part of the supervisor's repertoire as well. Outsiders and some parents can look at gifted education as a status-seeking endeavor, rather than just an optimal school learning experience that meets the rigor necessary for these children to be academically challenged and successful. The supervisor should have a formalized parent group that meets periodically throughout the school year as a means to network and answer parental questions and also as an opportunity to bring in speakers that address the challenges and struggles that many parents have to navigate raising a gifted child.

Some states require a written acceleration plan and a written individual-ized educational plan (WEP) to document either acceleration, or the learning needs of the child. Though paperwork can be cumbersome, it is important that all acceleration and pull out of any kind is documented. It also forces the team to meet on a regular basis to view progress and any concerns that might develop. A written plan can also be a protection for the child if he or she is pulled out. Some typical classroom teachers look at gifted education as a means to give additional homework or make up work if the student were pulled out for gifted instruction during the school day. The written plan can excuse the child for making up missed work, as he or she would have been given more challenging work in the pull-out session. This is another reason why the gifted intervention specialist needs to collaborate with the typical teacher to ensure the same material and the same scope and sequence is being followed.

Whenever any type of gifted education is considered for a student, the supervisor should include in team meetings the parents, the person who completed the evaluation, the general education classroom teacher, the prin-cipal or administrator, the gifted specialist, and the student when appropriate. By involving all of the players from the inception, a strong plan can be developed, and a student will be more likely to succeed academically and socially.

CASE STUDIES

- The parent of a gifted-and-talented student contacts you as the supervisor, as to the amount of homework that is given by the typical classroom teacher when the child is being pulled out for instruction by the gifted-and-talented intervention specialist. You contact the typical classroom teacher who shares that if the student is gifted, he or she should be able to keep up with the work load. What is your response?
- A parent contacts you requesting that his or her child be placed in the gifted pull-out classroom. When you review the assessment scores, you realize that the child does not qualify based upon the district policy. What is your next move?
- A team meeting is convened to determine if a child should be accelerated in math only. The regular middle school instructor is against the move as he or she has given the child a teacher-made assessment and the child did not display mastery of the test. The parent wants the child accelerated and claims before the meeting that the teacher does not like her child or their family. How do you resolve this dilemma?

REFERENCES

Brown, E. F., & Abernathy, S. H. (2009). Policy Implications at the State and District Level with RtI for Gifted Students. *Gifted Child Today*, Vol. 32, No. 3: 52–57.

Coleman, M. R., & Gallagher, J. (1995). State Identification Policies: Gifted Students from Special Populations. *Roeper Review*, Vol. 17: 268–275.

Hughes, C., & Rollins, K. (2009). "RtI for Nurturing Giftedness: Implications for the RtI School Based Team." *Gifted Child Today*, Vol. 32, No. 3.

Linn, B., & Shore, B. M. (2008). Critical Thinking. In J. A. Plucker & C. M. Callahan (eds.), *Critical Issues and Practices in Gifted Education* (pp. 155–166). Waco, TX: Prufrock Press.

McCollister, K., & Sayler, M. (2010). Lift the Ceiling: Increase Rigor with Critical Thinking Skills. *Gifted Child Today*, Vol. 33, No. 1: 41–47.

Paul, R., & Elder, L. (2008). *Critical Thinking Concepts and Tools*, 5th ed. Dillon, CA: Foundation for Critical Thinking.

Saylor, M. (2009). Gifted and Thriving: A Deeper Understanding of the Meaning of GT. In L. Shavinina (ed.), *The International Handbook on Giftedness* (pp. 215–230). Amsterdam, The Netherlands: Springer Science and Business Media.

Swartz, R. J., & Parks, S. (1994). *Infusing the Teaching of Critical and Creative Thinking into Elementary Instruction*. Pacific Grove, CA: Critical Thinking Press.

Tomlinson, C. (2003). *Fulfilling the Promise of the Differentiated Classroom: Strategies and Tools for Responsive Teaching*. Alexandria, VA: Association for Supervision and Curriculum Development.

Van-Tassel-Baska, J. (2003). *Curriculum Planning and Instructional Design for Gifted Learners*. Denver, CO: Love.

POINTS TO REMEMBER

- Response to Intervention should also be used in gifted identification.
- Children who have been identified as being gifted must have appropriate intervention and services or their IQ will fall back toward the mean score.
- Children identified as being gifted need the rigor of instruction increased with integration of critical thinking skills.
- Gifted instructors can instruct using a pull-out program or co-teaching with the classroom teacher.
- Acceleration by subject or grade level is a means to instruct gifted children. A protocol that is evidence based should be utilized to assist with the team decision on whether to accelerate or not accelerate a child.
- Differentiation is a means to meet the needs of all children within a classroom.
- A written education plan should be developed for children who are identified as gifted and talented. A written acceleration plan should be developed for children who may be subject- or grade-level accelerated. All plans should be reviewed at least annually or if there is a concern.

Chapter Five

The Twice-Exceptional Child

THEORY

The major emphasis of education is based on the premise that all children can learn, all should be challenged to achieve high standards, and all should have access to a rigorous, standards-based curriculum and evidence-based instructional strategies to ensure the individual success of every child. The twice-exceptional child exhibits giftedness and learning problems, presenting a unique blend of assets and deficits that may make learning a special challenge in those weaker areas.

Even if a student has a disability and is also gifted, he or she must be allowed to be challenged at his or her cognitive level with his or her intellectual peers so as to develop critical thinking skills and abstract reasoning skills (Baum & Owen, 2004). The delivery of instruction and materials may by challenging for the instructor, but with the appropriate adaptations in teaching strategies rather than modifying the content, the student should be able to fulfill the curricular goals and objectives (Schumaker & Lenz, 1999).

In the early 1980s, it was recommended that children be labeled by their behaviors rather than by the title *gifted and talented*. Looking at the behaviors allowed educators the opportunity to develop educational plans that matched a child's assets to their interests and abilities to ensure a more individualized approach to success (Renzulli, Reis, & Smith, 1981).

The definition of *gifted and talented* varies from state to state, which stereotypes the characteristics assigned to the group and does not take into account the individual assets, strengths, and weaknesses of the twice-exceptional child (Pereles, Omdal, & Baldwin, 2009). This stereotype of a label diminishes the recognition of individual behaviors or characteristics of the twice-exceptional learner. Thus, many schools tend to focus only on student deficits to improve year-end test scores over assets, and the twice-exception-al child loses out on the rigor of the gifted curriculum.

More than nine instructional strategies were developed by Marzano and colleagues (2001) to break down evidence-based teaching strategies that en-sure every child could be successful and reach their full potential. The strate-gies are listed from the highest success rate to the lowest success rate. These strategies are: identifying similarities and differences, summarizing and note taking, reinforcing effort and providing recognition, homework and practice, nonlinguistic representations, cooperative learning, setting objectives and providing feedback, generating and testing hypothesizes, and questions, cues, and advance organizers.

These strategies benefit all learners when used consistently during in-struction. The twice-exceptional child truly benefits from these research-based strategies because students with these strengths and weaknesses bene-fit from clear expectations, guidance, and an opportunity to problem solve while working in conjunction with the gifted standards (Landrum & Shaklee, 1988) and the Common Core. Pairing these strategies, the gifted standards and the Common Core, while using the tiered model of Response to Interven-tion (RTI) as a vehicle to intervene in a very fluid system will allow the twice-exceptional child much more success than has previously been offered in any classroom setting.

Focusing on behaviors with appropriate intervention using the RTI prob-lem-solving process may eliminate the need for any type of labeling of stu-dents in the future. Partnering with parents and collaborating as profession-als, looking at student data, benchmarking students for a baseline, applying the tiered interventions created from the data, progress monitoring and meet-ing as a team every six weeks, and intervening early should make most children successful.

The twice-exceptional child will benefit greatly from the RTI tiered mod-el because it addresses high-level instruction and appropriate remediation in the skill set deficit area(s). The student day could be based upon student need rather than a predetermined schedule put together a year earlier based upon teacher need and union contracts. The twice-exceptional child could have his or her needs met both behaviorally and academically by creating a school day based upon the RTI tiered model providing a challenging curriculum, while adapting the methodology of how the curriculum is presented so that instruction is based utilizing the student strengths rather than just focusing on the deficits and annual test scores. If the twice-exceptional child is chal-lenged the test scores will take care of themselves.

INTEGRATING THEORY INTO PRACTICE

As the director or supervisor of gifted programming for a district, one has to be cognizant that extra time needs to be devoted to planning to ensure the individual needs of each child with dual exceptionalities are met. Because this planning is a team effort, all players need to be included: the parents, the special needs intervention specialist, the gifted intervention specialist, the regular classroom teachers, and an administrator, and when appropriate, the student.

Specialists need to be brought onto the team if necessary. Some children with twice-exceptionality labels are on the autism spectrum and need a visual schedule and a concrete functional behavior plan to be successful. Others may need the gifted intervention specialist to go into the general classroom and work in conjunction with the classroom teacher because the child may not be comfortable leaving the room to work with the gifted intervention specialist somewhere else.

Children who are identified with learning disabilities as well as being considered gifted will need adaptations to the presentation of the curriculum to ensure they are being challenged. The difference between an adaptation and a modification is that with the adaptation, the presentation of material is presented with the student strengths in mind, while not changing the content. A modification would change the content so that the student would not be as challenged. This type of individualization may be challenging to the gifted intervention specialist, and he or she should consult with the special needs intervention specialist for ideas and for planning because that is their area of expertise.

Collaboration is going to be the only solution in ensuring that the twice-exceptional child is successful. This may be something new for the gifted intervention specialist because many who are veterans to the position are used to doing their own thing and working on their own created units. The supervisor or director needs to meet with the gifted intervention specialist to ensure that he or she is following the Common Core, as well as the same scope and sequence per subject area that the general classroom teacher is following.

Being on the same page as the classroom teacher is essential for the success of the child. If a child is on the autism spectrum, and re-enters the general classroom after a gifted pull-out session, he or she may feel extremely lost, which may trigger behaviors. If the subject is the same and there is a concrete behavior plan for re-entering the student, transition time should not be as traumatic for the student or the teacher. The use of video or social stories may also support the plan.

If a twice-exceptional child has a learning disability, the use of technology for the presentation of material by the gifted intervention specialist or the output of the student project or class work may be an adaption that will show the instructor what the student has learned.

The bottom line as a supervisor or a director of gifted education is to ensure that all of the needs of each child that is labeled twice exceptional are met. The spirit of IDEA and gifted standards wants each child to be looked at as an individual, and through collaboration of a team, including the parent and the student, a plan of success should be developed for the student to ensure that he or she is challenged with rigor. This challenge is not a once-a-year plan but needs to be looked at on a regular basis with progress monitoring data to ensure the student's continued success so as to work through the changes in curricular demands and the behavior(s) that might arise because of those changes.

CASE STUDIES

- A twice-exceptional child is participating in a gifted pull-out program. The student has behaviors that are interfering with the classroom instruction. The gifted-and-talented instructor wants the child removed permanently from the class because of the issues. The parent claims that the child's needs will not be satisfied without this pull-out instruction. Who do you side with when making your decision?
- The only pull-out program available in your district is in the area of language arts. An identified cognitive gifted-and-talented student with a specific learning disability in the areas of written expression and reading comprehension needs services. The parent would like the child to participate in this program, and the gifted-and-talented instructor does not believe that this would be an appropriate placement for this child. What is your response to both team members?
- A child identified as gifted and talented with high-functioning autism is participating in the gifted-and-talented pull-out classroom in language arts. The gifted-and-talented instructor is enhancing the core language arts curriculum but is not using the Common Core as the course of study. The student is not completing the classroom language arts class work because he claims he is getting language arts in the pull-out situation even though it is not the Common Core course of study. The school is recommending pulling the student from the gifted classroom, but the parent wants the child to remain. As the supervisor what is your response?

REFERENCES

Baum, S. & Owen, S. (2004). *To be Gifted and Learning Disabled: Strategies for Helping Bright Students with LD, ADHD, and More.* Mansfield, CT: Creative Learning Press.

Baum, S., Owen, S. V., & Dixon, J. (1991). *To Be Gifted and Learning Disabled: From Identification to Practical Intervention Strategies.* Mansfield Center, CT: Creative Learning Press.

Baum, S. M., Cooper, C. R., & Neu, T. W. (2001). Dual Differentiation: An Approach for Meeting the Curricular Needs of Gifted Students with Learning Disabilities. *Psychology in the Schools*, Vol. 38, No. 1: 477–490.

Cole, R. W. (2008). *Educating Everybody's Children: Diverse Teaching Strategies for Diverse Learners.* Alexandria, VA: Association for Supervision and Curriculum Development.

Coleman, M. R. (2005). Academic Strategies that Work for Gifted Students with Learning Disabilities. *Teaching Exceptional Children*, Vol. 38, No. 1: 28–32.

Colorado Department of Education. (2008). *Response to Intervention: A Practitioner's Guide to Implementation.* Denver, CO: Author.

Fox, L. H., Brody, L., & Tobin, D. (1983). *Learning Disabled Gifted Children: Identification and Programming.* Baltimore, MD: University Park Press.

Jeweler, S., Barnes-Robinson, L., Roffman Shevitz, B., & Weinfeld, R. (2008). Bordering on Excellence: A Teaching Tool for Twice-Exceptional Students. *Gifted Child Today*, Vol. 31, No. 2: 40–46.

King, E. W. (2005). Addressing the Social and Emotional Needs of Twice-Exceptional Students. *Teaching Exceptional Children*, Vol. 38, No. 1: 16–20.

Landrum, M. & Shaklee, B. (Eds.). (1998). *Pre-K–grade 12 Gifted Program Standards.* Washington DC: National Association for Gifted Children.

Lauchlan, F., & Boylle, C., (2007). Is the Use of Labels in Special Education Helpful? *Support for Learning*, Vol. 22, No. 1: 36–42.

Marzano, R. J., Pickering, D. J., & Pollock, J. E. (2001). *Classroom Instruction that Works: Research-Based Strategies for Increasing Student Achievement.* Alexandria, VA: Association for Supervision and Curriculum Development.

National Association of State Directors of Special Education. (2005). *Response to Intervention: Policy Considerations and Implementation.* Alexandria, VA: Author.

Nielson, M. E. (2002). Gifted Students with Learning Disabilities: Recommendations for Identification and Programming. *Exceptionality*, Vol. 10: 93–111.

Nielson, M. E., & Higgins, L. D. (2005). The Eye of the Storm: Service and Programs for Twice-Exceptional Learners. *Teaching Exceptional Children*, Vol. 38, No. 1: 8–15.

Pereles, D. A., Omdal, S., & Baldwin, L. (2009). Response to Intervention and Twice Exceptional Learners: A Promising Fit. *Gifted Child Today*, Vol. 32, No. 3: 40–51.

Renzulli, J. S., Reis, S. M., & Smith, L. H. (1981). *The Revolving Door Identification Model.* Nabsfuekd Center, CT: Creative Learning Press.

Ries, S. M., & Ruban, L. (2005). Services and Programs for Academically Talented Students with Learning Disabilities. *Theory into Practice*, Vol. 44: 148–159.

Schumaker, J., & Lenz, K. (1999). *Adapting Language Arts, Social Studies, and Science Materials for the Inclusive Classroom: Volume 3: Grades Six through Eight.* Reston, VA: ERIC Clearinghouse on Disabilities and Gifted Education.

Tomlinson, C. A. (2001). *How to Differentiate Instruction in Mixed-Ability Classrooms.* Upper Saddle River, NJ: Pearson Education.

Van Tassel-Baska, J. (1991). Serving the Disabled Gifted through Educational Collaboration. *Journal for the Education of the Gifted*, Vol. 14: 246–266.

Weinfeld, R., Barnes-Robinson, L., Jeweler, S., & Roffman Shevitz, B. (2006). *Smart Kids with Learning Difficulties: Overcoming Obstacles and Realizing Potential.* Waco, TX: Prufrock Press.

Yssel, N., Prater, M., & Smith, D. (2010). How Can Such a Smart Kid Not Get It? Finding the Right Fit for Twice-Exceptional Students in Our Schools. *Gifted Child Today*, Vol. 33, No. 1: 54–61.

POINTS TO REMEMBER

- Children can be identified as having a disability, as well as, being identified as gifted and talented.
- It is essential that children who are twice exceptional receive intervention
  for both their giftedness and their disability. This can be a challenge to
  intervene for staff members.
- Many gifted children and twice-exceptional children struggle with social
  skills. This deficit needs to be addressed to ensure a child is successful in
  all endeavors.

Chapter Six

English as a Second Language

THEORY

English as a second language (ESL), limited English proficiency (LEP), or English-language learner (ELL) instruction must be provided for all students with limited proficiency in English, who qualify according to individual district guidelines, which are based upon state guidelines. The legal basis for any English program is the landmark 1974 U.S. Supreme Court decision, *LAU vs. Nichols.*

This case began in 1971 in San Francisco, California, when approximately twenty-eight hundred Chinese students in the San Francisco School system did not speak English. About one thousand students did receive English intervention; however, the other eighteen hundred did not receive any assistance. This became a class action lawsuit with the allegation that the students were not provided equal educational opportunities, which is a violation of the Fourteenth Amendment.

The U.S. Supreme Court did not validate the Equal Protection Clause of this amendment, but rather relied on section 601 of the Civil Rights Act of 1964, which prohibits discrimination on the basis of race, color, or national origin. The U.S. Supreme Court ruled that the school system must ensure that LEP national origin minority students are able to benefit from an education conducted in English.

That action taken for these students is interpreted by each state a little differently, and by each school district even more so, with the end goal being that the student benefits by that interpretation.

Some districts, depending upon the population of LEP students, have classes established or require teachers to be bilingual within each K–12 building. Other school districts with smaller populations have tutors who pull those students out a few times per week to help support the student and the classroom teacher. Still other school districts that may be rural or highly agricultural may have migrant programs for student education to teach English, which is separate from their LEP program because of the transiency of the migrant student.

When a parent initially enrolls a student, a prelanguage survey should be a part of the general enrollment packet for all grade levels. This survey should include questions as to the language that the child was first taught or exposed to as a toddler. Questions should also inquire about the language spoken in the home and the amount of time the child has been in the United States. These questions are for *all* parents enrolling their child in school. An initial English survey on the form may inquire about the child's listening, speaking, reading, writing, and overall comprehension skills using the English language. Again this is for all students and potential students being enrolled in the school district.

These skills can be broken down in a checklist format from prefunctional to beginning to intermediate to advanced and finally to proficient. The checklist or survey is strictly the parent's input and should never be the *only* data used for assessment of English fluency. After perusing the application for enrollment, the district LEP instructor should administer some more formal assessment if there are questions regarding English fluency.

The prefunctional level usually is interpreted as students who may understand some isolated vocabulary, particularly school and social environmental words. Students at this level may comprehend high-frequency social conventions, simple short directions, or commands or questions. Students at this level rely heavily on nonverbal cues such as gestures and facial expressions. They may require frequent repetition and rephrasing to understand spoken language. They may be able to reply to simple questions, or they can ask one- or two-word questions without regard to intonation or grammatical structure.

A prefunctional English-speaking student may have some basic reading and/or prereading skills. They may be able to demonstrate an understanding of concepts in print. This would include front-to-back, top-to-bottom, or left-to-right comprehension of how the English written word is handled. Students at the prefunctional level may be able to track print or distinguish letters or words. They can model the act of reading by holding a book correctly and turning pages appropriately. Most students at this level use pictures or drawings to interpret the English language and their comprehension of spoken English. The prefunctional English-speaking student may imitate the act of writing, but their written text does not transmit a message.

The beginning English-speaking student may be able to vocalize and imitate the verbalizations of others but may still need much repetition to be successful. Their receptive language is stronger than their expressive language, but the actual construction of sentences is not complete or grammatically correct. The student's generated syntax reflects only simple texts in writing.

The intermediate level involves much more complicated speech. Students still may require some repetition. Students have acquired a bank of words and phrases that are appropriate to most situations that they may encounter daily. Their vocabulary may be somewhat restrictive and have many grammatical errors, but they can function for the most part in general conversations.

Reading proficiency may vary greatly between students who are characterized as functioning at the intermediate level of English construction. Students should be able to generate more complex coherent texts, yet with still many grammatical errors in syntax.

The advanced level of English fluency allows for day-to-day functioning in the general educational environment. Students still may struggle with idioms and slang but have established abstract concepts in their daily language communication. Writing in English has become more fluent, and fewer errors are made in the text. The student's thoughts and ideas, however, are adequately communicated.

The proficient level of speaking English allows the student to participate in academic discussions and can follow multilevel and complex directions in English without any difficulty. Students at the proficient level can read and comprehend most texts and can write and communicate both in a technical manner as well as by expressing clear thoughts in persuasive and argumentative writing. This is the stage where progress is closely monitored for the possible discontinuation of any type of intervention services because of the student's fluency in their acquisition of English, their second language.

Students are placed and monitored annually based upon some standardized English assessment that each state recommends and requires. In order for a student to receive services, continue services, or be exited from services, an annual standardized assessment must be completed to ensure adequate progress is being made in speaking, listening, reading, writing, and overall comprehension. A student is usually placed on the prefunctional to proficient scale annually based upon a numerical score taken from the assessment. This score determines the outcome of continued intervention for the next school year.

INTEGRATING THEORY INTO PRACTICE

Supervising a limited English program can be a challenge because many districts that are small do not offer too much service or intervention. Classroom teachers are overwhelmed on how to intervene or accommodate the child in their classroom. The LEP instructor or tutor may be only part time or very limited in his or her time to work one-on-one with students. Classroom teachers are concerned that if a child has been in the States for more than a year, their achievement on the state grade-level assessment may count and that will affect how the class ranks and possibly how the teacher's evaluation or publicized grade comes across in public or in the media.

Title money may be available in the district. Possibly hiring an assistant to the LEP instructor would help those classroom teachers who are over-whelmed. Looking at software that allows the new student to speak and listen to English may also assist the student, as well as the overwrought teacher.

Classroom teachers may need to be trained in how to create a welcoming environment in their classroom. The instructor needs to learn how to pronounce the student's name correctly. He or she should offer one-on-one assistance whenever possible. Having a Title assistant could also help with this one-on-one time, too. A visual picture schedule may be a good way to assist the student in understanding the structure of the classroom and add to the new student's comfort level. Having a peer partner creates a way to include the student in the classroom culture. Also assigning different lunch buddies and recess pals may all help the new member of the class.

The classroom teacher may need assistance in including the LEP student in the classroom discussion. The teacher needs to be aware of the child's culture and some of the hidden nuances from that culture. Homework and class work may be simplified or modified for the student. Meeting the parent, with an interpreter if necessary, is a good way to establish parent and student rapport. The younger the child, the faster the immersion into the language takes place. The classroom teacher needs to be predictable, structured, and concrete in giving directions, using gestures to assist in communication.

The Title assistant can also assist the teacher and student with organization and provide different opportunities and additional examples of language fundamentals and usage within the classroom. At the secondary level, the LEP teacher or tutor tends to be in more of a survival mode in helping students pass classes and earn Carnegie credits or units toward graduation. The instructor should have word walls posted, as well as many visuals. Texts should be recorded, and the student should be able to take the CD home for practice. Role-playing, read aloud, and modified work and chunking are a must for survival. Giving pass or fail grades are important and modifying the amount of homework given every night may help in the language acquisition for the new student.

The most difficult part of the supervision of the LEP program is realizing that every student's language acquisition must be individualized. There are no one-size-fits-all recipes for success. National Honor Society students can be used as tutors to earn volunteer hours, or classroom peers may assist the success of a program and make the new student feel more comfortable.

Mathematics is not usually as difficult as the reading and language area for most students.

The LEP instructor may want to initiate a parent group or network parents to help the families assimilate into the community and the classroom. Encouraging English to be spoken in the home is another way to help language acquisition, as is using television to understand some of the language being spoken. Even if parents and students speak English for an hour a night, there will definitely be growth in the student's acquisition.

Lastly, offering teacher training prior to an instructor having a new member in the classroom will help the teacher. Possibly referring the classroom teacher to Web sites that give examples of how to work with students who do not speak English will help them in their transition to work with an LEP student. Lastly, if the LEP instructor develops a paper trail or individualized English-learning plans for each student, the progress will be easier to follow, and everyone will note additional language growth.

Any communication, even permission to work with the LEP instructor, should be in the child's native language. Title money will allow for paid translations to be contracted, which ensures that the parents are aware of what is being offered. A copy of the letter in English should also be included to ensure the intent of the letter if the translated letter is in error.

School systems need to take the LEP program very seriously because it is federal law. Many times the programs appear more as an added initiative rather than a strong, legitimate program. Some state departments of education look at LEP students as a subgroup, which could impact state scores for a specific district. Sometimes that information is necessary for central administration to ensure there are appropriate resources available to make this population successful.

The LEP instructor or supervisor may want to jointly present a program to Rotary group service organizations or chamber of commerce groups and boards of education to elicit volunteers to assist the student at home or the family in the community. There are always willing adults in a community who want to volunteer, but they must be informed of the needs that the school programs may have or the assistance that is needed.

Keep in mind that the students who are LEP are the fastest-growing segment of the U.S. student population. Schools need to be cognizant of the national achievement gap between English-speaking students and LEP students. Statewide assessments across the country are becoming much more language based, and students must be able to comprehend what is being asked of them in order to display what they truly know academically. The No Child Left Behind Act (2001) expects all children to be proficient and for the achievement gap to close. The supervisor of the LEP program must be an advocate for the program by making presentations and understanding the needs of the instructor and the typical classroom teacher. By assisting the

professional adults in being comfortable and knowledgeable, the students
will end up being the winners in the classroom.

CASE STUDIES

- As the supervisor of the LEP program, a typical classroom teacher contacts you complaining that her new student is only getting twenty minutes
  of pull out from the LEP instructor every week. You contact the LEP
  instructor and that is all that can be offered based upon his or schedule.
  There is a hiring freeze, and hours cannot be increased. What is your
  response to both professionals? How do you meet the needs of the child?
- You receive a phone call from a parent of a student with LEP. He or she
  has a five-year-old whom they feel is gifted and talented. The parent wants
  to accelerate the child to first grade even though the grade level may not
  be appropriate. The family is returning to their native country the following school year, and culturally that would be an appropriate age to have
  this child in first grade in the native country. The parents do not want the
  child behind when they return home in a year. The child is assessed and is
  gifted and could be appropriate for first grade but is very immature for her
  age. What is your decision?
- You receive a phone call from the typical classroom teacher that he or she
  is sure that the LEP student has special needs. The child has been in the
  states for five months. The teacher wants the child assessed or moved back
  to the previous grade because he or she cannot master the curriculum.
  What is your response, and how do you assist the student?

REFERENCES

Cummins, J. (2003). Reading and the Bilingual Student: Fact and Friction. In G. G. Garcia
    (ed.), *English Learning Learners in the Mainstream Classroom* (pp. i–ix). Portsmouth, NH:
    Heinemann.
DeJong, E. (2004). After Exit: Academic Achievement Patterns of Former English Language
    Learners. *Education Policy Analysis Archives*, Vol. 12, No. 50: 1–18.
Olson, L. (2000). Learning English and Learning America: Immigrants in the Center of the
    Storm. *Theory into Practice*, Vol. 39, No. 4: 196–202.
Pu, Chang. (2010). Rethinking Literacy Instruction to Non-LEP/ESL-Labeled Language Mi-
    nority Students. *Literacy Teaching and Learning*, Vol. 15, Nos. 1 & 2: 137–155.

POINTS TO REMEMBER

- English as a second language is also referred to as limited English proficiency.
- All school districts must have a plan to service these children as it is a
  federal mandate.

- Section 601 of the Civil Rights Act of 1964 prohibits discrimination on the basis of race, color, or natural origin. The LEP program falls under this determination.
- When a child is initially enrolled in a district, a language survey should be completed by the parent to determine if a student needs LEP services.
- There are varied service delivery models from tutoring to pull out to actual classrooms that are bilingual.
- English is assessed annually and children cannot be dismissed by a district until they score above the fluent and proficient levels.

Chapter Seven

Dyslexia

THEORY

Dyslexia can be difficult to diagnose, and many school systems are not comfortable using that word. Schools prefer the terminology of reading disability in the area of decoding or comprehension. The rationale for many schools is that they are not adequately prepared to teach with a multisensory approach, which has proven to be successful with children who have this disorder.

The International Dyslexia Association in 2002 developed a detailed definition of dyslexia and are advocating that this definition be utilized in school systems on a national level. The definition is inclusive and states, "Dyslexia is a specific learning disability that is neurobiological in origin. It is characterized by difficulties with accurate and/or fluent word recognition and by poor spelling and decoding abilities. These difficulties typically result from a deficit in the phonological component of language that is often unexpected in relation to other cognitive abilities and the provision of effective classroom instruction. Secondary consequences may include problems with reading comprehension and reduced reading experience that can impede growth of vocabulary and background knowledge" (Shaywitz, 2003).

One myth that continues to surface is that people with dyslexia see letters and numbers backward and that reversals are common to this disorder. Tendencies for this disorder can be recognized very early in child development. A preschooler's phonological aptitude can predict reading skills three years in advance of beginning reading aptitude (Bradley & Bryant, 1980). Shaywitz (2003) believes that a successful program for children having dyslexia utilizes an early program intervention for the weaknesses and accommodations to address the strengths and cognitive skills that a child may posses.

A diagnosis for young children should take into consideration phonology awareness, names and sounds of letters, segmentation, vocabulary, both receptive and expressive, listening comprehension, and basic reading of real and nonsense words with comprehension as a part of the process. There are many tests on the market that measure these attributes. None of the tests are perfect, and all have a degree of error.

Once a child has been identified, then the most important component of the process is the type of service offered to assist the child in overcoming aspects of the disorder. There have been many brain studies completed on children before and after an intervention has been implemented. If the correct early intervention is used, and early is significant, then the brain displays actual physical changes that coincide with the child's success in reading.

Besides the individualized intervention, the core program for all children should be reviewed. Reading programs for *all* children should include scientific evidence that the program is effective. One of the critiques should have been completed by the National Reading Panel that should include explicit script teaching in phonetics and phonetic awareness. Fluency should be encrypted in the program also.

If a child is diagnosed with dyslexia, then placing the child in a special education reading classroom with larger numbers will not close the gap between the student and his or her other grade-level classmates. The gap will continue to get bigger as the child ages. Children with dyslexia need a scripted multisensory approach to reading that is evidence based. School systems shy away from this approach because it is initially very expensive to train the intervention instructors. However, this is the only program that has been researched, has been proven to work, and makes a difference in the lives of young children.

There is now in many states a third-grade reading guarantee going into effect stating that if a third grader is not reading at or above his or her grade level, parents must be notified in writing in the fall, and the child will be retained to remediate the problem. If a child is diagnosed with dyslexia, the only method of correcting that disorder is through a multisensory individually scripted program for that child. If the child is not dyslexic, then an evidence-based scripted reading program should be utilized to ensure that reading growth is markedly improved.

INTEGRATING THEORY INTO PRACTICE

As a director or supervisor it is very critical to assess the reading programs used by the intervention specialists in the district, as well as to evaluate the reading program in the district's core curriculum. If the reading program in the core is not evidence based and does not have a scripted phonics program, then many children who struggle with decoding may be having difficulty because the appropriate skill set has not been taught in their reading class. Some children need that direct instruction to master phonemic awareness.

In many districts, intervention specialists are left to fend on their own for materials. If a group gets together with the director or supervisor, it is not uncommon to see that every specialist is doing their own thing with the instruction and that they have not been provided any guidance or evidence-based scripted curriculum to assist the students in closing their individual reading gap with their classmates.

A leader supervising the department must ensure that all intervention specialists have a scripted evidence-based program that guarantees reading improvement or the students will fall further and further behind. This can be an expensive venture initially, but long term the pay off is critical for the success of the student and the success of the intervention specialist. The individualized educational plan (IEP) should be specific regarding the increased number of words read per minute in a cold read and stating the number of miscues that will be accepted.

Writing IEPs that specifically ensure that a child is improving annually is ethically the right thing to do to ensure a child's success. However, if the district has not provided a researche-based reading program for all intervention specialists that is appropriate to the age level and skill set of the children they are serving, then writing a goal so specifically will set up the specialist for failure in meeting the annual goals.

There are so many facets to supervising a special needs program that it is essential for the director to prioritize those concerns that will make the most positive impact on the greatest number of students within a short period of time. It is also a good idea once the director or supervisor has a good understanding of the district to have an outside university or knowledgeable group audit the system to see where the strengths and weaknesses may be hiding within the programs.

The audit results are public record and the supervisor must be prepared for some possible negative publicity involved in the reporting of the results. If the supervisor plans to utilize those weaknesses as a spring board for developing a strategic plan of improvement, then that negative could be turned around in a hurry. It is beneficial to form a committee to develop those departmental goals from the evaluation to ensure ownership by the district. The director should include intervention specialists, psychologists, speech and language therapists, motor team representation, and a few parents. That type of team can really make a positive difference within a district that might have been struggling in the past.

Reading is fundamental to survival in today's society and with today's technology. Recognizing and identifying children with dyslexia can turn a child's life around for the long term. Too often, districts get hung up on labels and terminology rather than services. It truly should not matter what label is given to a disability, but rather what appropriate research-based services and strategies are being used to assist the child in finding success. It is the director's ethical obligation to ensure that all children are getting the necessary services that will make them successful during the school year and for life.

CASE STUDIES

- A child has been having difficulty reading, and the parent has requested a multifactored evaluation. The team claims they are implementing response to intervention, and the intervention appears to be working because the child seems to be making progress. The team denies the testing request on the grounds that the child is making progress with the intervention. The parent contacts you as the supervisor. How do you resolve this stale mate?
- A child has been diagnosed with dyslexia and has been receiving evidence-based multisensory instruction. The child is improving and is not showing regression. The parent has requested an extended school year so the child does not regress over the summer. The team does not have evidence of regression over school holiday vacations. The parent calls you to resolve the situation. He or she claims that the school was slow to identify his or her child, and therefore owes the child an extended school year. What is your decision and why?
- A parent discusses the possibility of dyslexia with his or her child's teacher at November conferences. The teacher had asked the child if he or she saw numbers backward and the child responded "no." The teacher told the parent that therefore the student cannot be dyslexic. The parent contacts you as the director to participate in a meeting with the teacher. What is your response to the parent and the teacher at that meeting?

REFERENCES

Bradley L., & Bryant, P. (1983). Categorizing Sounds and Learning to Read—A Casual Connection. *Nature*, Vol. 301: 419–21.

Hanushuk, E. A., Kain, J. F., & Rivkin, S. G. (1998). *Does Special Education Raise Academic Achievement for Students with Disabilities?* Working Paper 6690, Cambridge, MA: National Bureau of Economic Research.

Lyon, G. Reid. (2002). International Dyslexia Association meeting. Washington, DC.

Shaywitz, S. (2003). *Overcoming Dyslexia*. New York: Vintage Books.

POINTS TO REMEMBER

- "Dyslexia is a specific learning disability that is neurobiological in origin. It is characterized by difficulties with accurate and/or fluent word recognition and by poor spelling and decoding abilities. These difficulties typically result from a deficit in the phonological component of language that is often unexpected in relation to other cognitive abilities and the provision of effective classroom instruction" (International Dyslexia Association as cited in Shaywitz, 2003).
- Treatment for dyslexia needs to be a systematic, multisensory, evidence-based program.
- Magnetic resonance imaging (MRI) tests have been completed and children who have had the correct treatment for dyslexia show a medical difference before and after the multisensory, scripted, evidence-based strategy and intervention.

Chapter Eight

Developmental Delays

THEORY

Developmental delays are a kinder or politically correct method of using the term *mental retardation*, which the federal law utilizes in the diagnostic process. This population has evolved from the terminology of educable mentally retarded to developmentally delayed. Labels mean nothing other than it is essential and necessary per the law to have a label to receive specially designed services and instruction.

This group of individuals used to be considered the hidden population in that they were not identified or labeled as different until school age and then merged quietly back into society without any label but with lower self-esteem. Though the times have changed, this population of students still lag behind their peers, have lower expectations put upon them, are not taking advantage of their academic opportunities, and are more likely to drop out of school (Aron & Loprest, 2012).

Historically, children with developmental disabilities were segregated in self-contained classrooms. If a child was lucky they were allowed to participate in special area classes such as physical education, art or music, and home economics. These children had no expectations put upon them, and this type of mainstreaming was considered a method of socialization for the children though they were often ostracized within the typical classroom. A turning point in schools treating children this way occurred in 1973.

Before the passage of Section 504, only one in about five children with identified disabilities attended public school, and many of these children were banned from a public education and were placed in separate facilities or institutions (Aron & Loprest, 2012).

Section 504 of the Rehabilitation Act of 1973 banned schools from receiving federal money if they discriminated against people with disabilities. This discrimination took years to change in local districts, and it is still occurring in most schools, only a bit more subtly. With the passage of the Individuals with Disabilities Education Act (IDEA), children now have better access to the general curriculum, although it still tends to be a fight to have children included in the general curriculum classes.

Though children with delays are included more in the general education system, the question now arises as to how successful these children are performing and functioning with this exposure to the general curriculum. Special education is now being held accountable for the education—key word being education—of this population. The passage of No Child Left Behind (2001) changed the educational game. Assessment and data from the assessment began to drive instruction and education.

The National Assessment of Educational Progress (NAEP), which is internationally normed, has started assessing the success of all children in school. In 2009, reading was assessed based upon this instrument, and sixty-four percent of children identified with disabilities tested below basic proficiency. Other subtests in math and other subjects showed the same disparity across the board (Center for Educational Policy, 2009). Factors for this disparity were blamed upon cognitive ability, parental expectations, absenteeism, and discipline issues (Loprest & Maag, 2003).

Other studies have depicted that once a child with a disability is finished with high school, the transition process into adult life has been very difficult for the individual. Students who graduate have little or no postsecondary training and have difficulty finding employment—skilled or unskilled—and overall satisfaction and contribution to civil engagement within their community is diminished compared to their typical peers (Wehman, 2006). As adults, many of these students get involved in the adult justice system. Due to these findings, transition planning is now a critical part of the individualized educational plan (IEP) process beginning at age fourteen.

Involving the student in the IEP process as he or she reaches adolescence makes a difference in how involved the student is in his or her educational process. The more involved the student and his or her parents are in the IEP and educational process, the better the student's odds are for finding success and satisfaction long term after graduation.

Schools that appear to be successful in the assessment of skills tend to include the students in typical classes. The exposure to content is critical in measuring how successful a child's education and skill set will be in the future. The children contained in special education classrooms miss the content exposure and fail to recognize information on the state assessments.

Many states are addressing this issue by expanding the National Common Core Curriculum by extending those standards to include more practicality in real-world situations. For example, instead of finding geometric shapes in mathematics on paper, the student may be asked to look at specific shapes and find those shapes in real-life structures. Extending the standards without watering down the curriculum will assist students with developmental delays to be more successful later on in life. Exposure to the same content with different methodology will tend to make students with disabilities better adjusted in the adult world.

INTEGRATING THEORY INTO PRACTICE

As a supervisor or director it is essential to utilize the best professional development opportunities available for teachers. Many of the intervention specialists who are older than thirty-five years were not involved in learning how to ensure accountability for the academic success of their children. These teachers were trained in more of an overview of disabilities and services rather than becoming highly qualified in select areas of study.

This presents a problem for these teachers: not understanding and being overwhelmed by the new expectations coming down on public education. Most teachers studied special education to help and make life better for their students. In many instances, this did not include specific academic skills and strategies to help students with disabilities meet the requirements and expectations of the Common Core curriculum being handed down on a national level.

As the manager of special education programs, one has to stay current in the legislation being passed both on national and state levels. This legislation then must be passed down to intervention specialists with the expectation and assistance of some professional development. If an instructor feels comfortable and not overwhelmed, it is certain that the student will find success.

Education in 2012 is like the "perfect storm" for veteran and all staff members. The bar continues to rise nationally and locally for students and teachers. Inclusion can become a struggle as typical teachers may not want students with special needs in their classroom or on their roster, so that the instructors are not held accountable for one year's growth of educational progress in that subject area. Therefore, the typical teacher must also be involved in the training of new standards and how as a school system those standards will be maintained and achieved. This responsibility of education again falls on the director or supervisor of special education.

Writing standards-based IEPs will generate and promote learning in the typical classroom. Having instructors trained in intensive skills or strategies in specific content disciplines will ensure that the special education instructors are capable of teaching the curriculum that is now required. Literacy is emphasized in the Common Core curriculum. How typical teachers and intervention specialists collaborate will make a strong impact on how the student masters the content. There is now emerging research on how to teach content to severely disabled students, which had not been around before because it was never considered.

As a director or supervisor the ever-changing legislation can be daunting in understanding how to implement the educational requirements. It is essential that ethically one does not lose sight as to why one became a supervisor in the first place and that should always be for the success academically and socially of the children being served by the district. Parent involvement and building a sense of trust with the family assists greatly in the success of the student.

Parental and student involvement will give the IEP purpose and drive the goals and objectives to ensure that the student is successful both educationally and socially. As a supervisor or director, child advocacy is the purpose and foundation of the position, explaining to the instructors and building administrators that special education is not a place but a service that an entire team must lead and partake in to ensure the success of all children both academically and postsecondary. The other point to drive home is reminding these professionals that all children can and should be able to learn in spite of the assessments, expectations, and fear and negativity because of the fear and accountability of the adults within the school setting.

CASE STUDIES

- An instructor sends you an email complaining that a parent will not let his or her child help with the recycling program during school hours. This program is a part of the child's transition plan on the IEP. The parent refuses to have the goal removed from the plan but does not want his or her child to leave the classroom during what should be classroom instruction. How do you respond as the supervisor?
- The intervention specialist is writing an IEP, which includes some functional curriculum. The parent only wants academic goals on the IEP and does not want any functional curriculum given during the instructional day because the parent feels enough of that type of thing is done at home. The rest of the class leaves the classroom and participates in the functional curriculum. How do you resolve the situation and ensure there is appropriate supervision? Hiring staff is not an option.
- The developmental program that is your supervisory responsibility moves to a career center for the junior and senior year in high school. A parent of a child who has developmental delays wants their child to remain at the high school totally included and not to go to the career center. As the

supervisor you know that the student will not be receiving an appropriate education in a total inclusion setting. What do you do?

REFERENCES

Aron, L., & Loprest, P. (2012). Disability and the Education System. *The Future of Children*, Vol. 22, No. 1: 97–122.

Center for Educational Policy. http://www.gao.gov/new.items/d09286.pdf. Retrieved 10/15/2012.

Loprest, P., & Maag, E. (2003). *The Relationship between Early Disability Onset and Education and Employment.* Washington, DC: Urban Institute.

Wehman, P. (2006). *Life beyond the Classroom: Transition Strategies for Young People with Disabilities.* Baltimore, MD: Brooks Publishing.

POINTS TO REMEMBER

- Section 504 of the Rehabilitation Act of 1973 prohibited federal funding for school systems that discriminated against children who had developmental delays.
- Children need to be included as much as possible in the typical classroom so that they are exposed to the core content.
- Standards-based individualized educational plans need to be written so that children who have developmental delays can access the Common Core curriculum.

Chapter Nine

Emotional Disturbance

THEORY

Being diagnosed as having an emotional disturbance is a serious label to place on a child, and the team of educators and parents must look at all types of interventions prior to completing an assessment or referring the child for a multifactored evaluation. The team must consider if the behaviors have occurred over a long period of time, which is more than just one school year. The team must also consider if the behaviors that are occurring are to a marked degree meaning that the behaviors are happening across school settings and at home and that the behaviors are adversely affecting school performance. This means that the behaviors are preventing the child from learning the curriculum, and he or she is falling behind because of the behaviors not allowing the child to participate or access the Common Core.

The school or personal history of the child needs to be examined to ensure that the behaviors are not a reaction to a divorce, a death in the family, or the child being bullied. Utilizing the Response to Intervention (RTI) framework, the child's behaviors must be examined closely. An observation by someone other than the teacher is a good start to collect data (Howard, 2003).

The observation should consider the structure of the classroom. This can be interpreted as classroom routines, structured transitions, classroom rules, and overall expectations for the students. As the instructor begins to teach are the rules being followed consistently by all students? Does the instructor reinforce the rules during the instruction, as well as ensure that the paraprofessionals follow the rules during their interaction with the student?

The observer must watch what is triggering the behavior or the antecedent of the concern (Horner & Sugal, 1999–2000). When the student begins to exhibit the behavior, what is the adult response to the behavior, and does that response. verbal or nonverbal, escalate the student behavior? In other words, does the adult response appear appropriate for the circumstance or is there an overreaction that might escalate the behavior of concern? This is essential in determining if the behavior is being reinforced without the instructor even being aware that he or she is exacerbating the behavior.

The consequence for the behavior must also be considered. Is the given consequence natural to the situation? This can be interpreted as, do the behaviors directly relate to the consequence, and is there a learning piece to the consequence so that it is not just a punitive reaction? This antecedent, behavior, and consequence (ABC) must be taken into consideration by the observer, so that the behavior can be isolated within the cause-and-effect relationship if a strong plan is to be developed by the team.

Prior to the observation of the student, the observer must have a strong understanding of the teacher's tolerance level for background noise and background movement. This may have a strong influence on the structure or lack of structure within the overall setting of the classroom. The instructor's tone and quality of instruction may also be a trigger for the given behavior.

The observer should also note if the classroom rules are posted, the number of rules for the classroom, and if the rules are reinforced consistently throughout the classroom instruction. The instructor should also have separate behavior plans for the children if they have behaviors that are inconsistent with the classroom regulations. The observation is the first step in establishing those plans.

The demeanor of the classroom must be noticed by the observer. Do students carry on side conversations during instruction? Is there much student movement during seat time, do the students raise their hand to participate or do they talk out, and does the instructor tolerate inappropriate behavior and continue teaching? These are essential concerns because the instructor must model the behavioral expectations of the classroom. If a child is in a special needs classroom, the goal would be to have the student included in the typical class. If the instructor accepts behaviors that will not be accepted in a typical classroom, then the instructor is inadvertently setting up the student for failure when he or she might be included in the typical classroom down the road.

Once the behavior has been isolated, it is then important to determine the rationale or purpose for the student acting out in the classroom. Is the behavior for attention or an issue with frustration over the work expectation or just an inability for the student to communicate effectively? Once the observation is complete, the team needs to reconvene and examine the behaviors and develop a functional behavior assessment (FBA). The rationale behind an FBA is to determine what factors and positive behavioral supports are necessary to extinguish the given behavior and to engage the student in a positive learning environment (O'Neill et al., 1997).

When completing an observation using time intervals, it is sometimes a good method to document the class period and the activity and how it relates to the time in the classroom. As an instructor it is very easy to lose one's perspective when the teacher is so close to the behaviors on a daily basis. It is also extremely important to document the routine, as to where and when the behavior occurs and which person or people are involved with the problematic interaction (Freeman et al., 1999). As an observer takes notes, it is also important to document what the possible function of the behavior is for the student so that when developing a functional behavior plan that function can be taken into consideration.

Once the individualized educational plan (IEP) team has completed the FBA, the team then needs to develop a workable functional behavior plan for the student using the data taken from the assessment. An implementation plan hopefully provides strategies to manage the behaviors within the classroom. The plan should use positive behavior support for the student, as well as provide a measurable documentation section to determine the success of the plan. Working with behaviors is a trial-and-error proposition. However, with a strong observation and behavior assessment, the needed data will be present to increase the possibility for the plan and the student to be successful.

INTEGRATING THEORY INTO PRACTICE

As a supervisor, when developing a classroom for identified emotionally disturbed children, there are a number of things to consider before implementation. A strong mental health consideration is necessary to achieve optimum success. Having a mental health counselor, with written parent permission, to see children individually and in a group session to practice social skills will ensure that the program is working through the issues and not just the behaviors that have been identified as problematic. Strong programs also have the instructor and mental health professionals work with the parents to ensure consistency between home and school. Sometimes parents just need an outlet to communicate the home issues, receiving positive suggestions for dealing effectively with those issues. Having conferences just in the fall will not enhance communication nor impact the home environment.

The instructor and staff must be trained in therapeutic handling of students in crisis. This needs to be a trained team effort by a certified instructor. The federal government recently has published rulings on seclusion and restraint criteria. Each state is interpreting these criteria, so knowledge of state requirements as a supervisor is essential. Seclusion should never be used as a punishment.

Individual behavior assessments and plans should be a critical part of the IEP with an identified emotionally disturbed child. The plans must be measurable so that success can be defined by observable data. All paraprofessionals must be trained to implement the behavior plans in a structured, consistent manner and be able to collect consistent data.

The instructor must be trained in positive behavioral supports so that the interventions are not all negative in their implementation. An individual crisis plan should be part of the behavior plan, and all staff members need to be trained in what that looks like with each student. The instructor needs to be self-aware of how he or she interacts with the students. Each student may have a different methodology on how they need to be treated to achieve optimum success.

There also needs to be some general classroom rules that all students and staff follow. Consistency is key if a classroom routine is to be established. In working with at-risk populations, many times the adults forget that students need to be taught how to understand transitions and routines. Too often the structures of the classroom are not taught except in kindergarten. When working with an at-risk population, the routines, transitions, and structures must be taught and reinforced on a regular basis.

Many behavior programs have point or level systems to assist with classroom structure, as well as positive behavior supports that are reinforcing to the child. Implementing natural and logical consequences connected to the behavior tends to be more successful than punitive measures. Natural consequences can be a learning tool for the student if utilized correctly. Teaching self-management strategies as well as using positive peer support can also impact a child or decrease a behavior effectively.

Lastly, curriculum must be appropriate to the core that the child will ultimately return to in the typical classroom. Many times the course of study in a special needs classroom is watered down or forgotten as the instructor is working just on behavior. Finally, when the behaviors are in check, the student starts being included back in the classroom but is effectively lost because the special needs teacher did not keep the child's skill set current as it compares to other students in the typical classroom.

If a child feels unsuccessful, the behaviors will begin to reappear, and the child will not be successful in the typical classroom. Inclusion back to the typical classroom is the overall goal for every student. Many times without realizing it, the classroom teacher develops such a comfort zone for the child that he or she does not want to leave the special education setting. A supervisor must work with the special needs instructor to ensure that the student feels safe, but not so comfortable that they forget the goal of the program, which is to get all students back into the mainstream of a typical classroom and schedule.

CASE STUDIES

- As the supervisor of this program for children with emotional disturbance, a parent at an IEP meeting requests mental health services during the school day. Your district does not have the money to support this request, although you agree that the child needs this service. What is your response?
- You overhear an intervention specialist teacher in the lounge who works with children with emotional disturbance complaining that all of her cases involve poor parenting and that the children are really delinquents. You speak to the teacher about her comments, and you receive a grievance the next day stating that you were eavesdropping on a private conversation. What is your response? How do you impact the teacher attitude when he or she has tenure?
- You receive a call from a parent stating that his or her child is missing lunch daily because of detentions. When you investigate the complaint, you learn the student does get to eat lunch but not in the cafeteria if he or she acts out. Consequences were written into the behavior plan but were not spelled out specifically to the parent. The parent refuses to come in and meet with the teacher and requests the IEP be discontinued. What is your response?

REFERENCES

Freeman, R. (2012). University of Kansas, Lawrence, Kansas, 66045. Retrieved October 13, 2012, from http://www.specialconnections.ku.edu.

Freeman, R. L., Smith, C. L., Tieghi-Benet, M. (2003). Promoting Implementation Success Through the Use of Continuous Systems-Level Assessment Strategies. *Journal of Positive Behavior Interventions*, Vol. 5: 66–70.

Horner, R. H., & Sugal, G. (1999–2000). Special Issue: Functional Behavior Assessment. *Exceptionality*, Vol. 8, No. 3: 145–230.

Howard, W. L. (2003). *Exceptional Children: An Introduction to Special Education.* Upper Saddle River, NJ: Pearson Education, Inc.

O'Neill, R. E., Horner, R. H., Albin, R. W., Sprague, J. R., Storey, K., & Newton, J. S. (1997). *Functional Assessment and Program Development for Problem Behavior: A Practical Handbook*, 2nd ed. Pacific Grove, CA: Brooks.

POINTS TO REMEMBER

- Children with an emotional disturbance must display behaviors over a long period of time, to a marked degree, and these behaviors must have an adverse reaction on the child in question.
- A child who is socially maladjusted or has been traumatically impacted by divorce or death cannot qualify for these services.

- The classroom environment and the behavior plan should have a positive impact on the child's behavior. A functional behavior assessment must be completed prior to developing a behavior plan for a child.

Chapter Ten

Transition

THEORY

Transition services has many facets from preschool to kindergarten, elementary school to middle school, middle school to high school, and high school to the world of postsecondary education and/or work. The transition between grade levels tends to be more difficult for the parent than the child because the parents have to trust a different adult than who they have grown accustomed to and trusted during the student's tenure in that school setting.

As a supervisor it is important to provide consistency between these transition periods to ensure that the student is comfortable and that the parent feels supported during these grade-level changes. It is not necessary during these transition meetings to rewrite an individualized educational plan (IEP), but rather have the parent meet the important players in the next school. These players should include an administrator, a special needs teacher, the special education supervisor, and a guidance counselor. This provides the parent with a connection and a point person(s) to ask all of their questions regarding the next school year. The special education supervisor is the consistency between buildings.

In secondary education, many students with disabilities become lost between high school and vocational pursuits or postsecondary education (National Longitudinal Transition Study-2, 2005). This lack of focus between school age and adulthood presents a few issues. Students in high school adhere to the Individuals with Disabilities Act (IDEA) and have an IEP with a strong measurable transition plan driving the goals and objectives on the IEP. Postsecondary involves the American Disabilities Education Act (ADA), which forces the students and parents to navigate an entirely different system of bureaucracy. Under IDEA, all students regardless of their disability must receive a quality education with educators advocating for the student. Under ADA, the student must advocate for himself or herself.

Research indicates that students in secondary education should be actively involved in the IEP process and begin to practice self-advocacy in school, which should be a safe setting and a strong safety net for the student (National Longitudinal Transition Study-2, 2005). It also allows the student to become aware of his or her own strengths and weakness so as to better advocate. Students should be active in setting goals and assist with the writing of their IEP. This self-determination has proven to assist students after they graduate.

Special education instructors will need professional development in the attributes of self-determination and how to utilize different teachable moments throughout the school year to reinforce those attributes. Traits like making appropriate choices, problem solving, goal setting, self-awareness, and self-advocacy are all characteristics of self-determination. Instructors can weave these traits into their daily teaching practice and assist the student in finding independence as different real situations occur in the high school setting.

There are ways to get the student more involved in the IEP process. The high school student could facilitate his or her own IEP with the intervention specialist providing the necessary details. The student can refer back to the IEP periodically to ensure that what is happening with his or her support system is matching up to the goals and objectives on the IEP. Drafts of the IEP, in advance of the conference, can be sent home with the student to discuss possible changes or alterations to the document prior to the conference. If there is a strong trust relationship between home and school, the actual conference can be more of a signing formality with the student sharing what is going to happen on the IEP, rather than adults negotiating goals and objectives and accommodations at the actual annual review.

Secondary schools can help with the transition process by being the conduit between the student and the postsecondary institution. Most universities want a current multifactored evaluation within the last twelve months in order to put into play accommodations under ADA, which would be a 504 plan. If the school becomes responsible for ensuring the testing is up to date, this saves money for the family, as well as expedites the admissions process.

Once accepted, it is the responsibility of the student to not only self-advocate but also seek out the support necessary for his or her own success. At a secondary school, implementing modifications, changing the curriculum, and providing the necessary support is given with an effective, well-written IEP. Postsecondary modifications and curriculum changes are not part of the process. Only accommodations become a part of the 504 or advocacy plan (Hanover Research, 2012).

Students with more severe disabilities need to use the transition plan as a means of interest inventories and actual vocational experiences with a job coach. Most outside agencies will not participate actively in this venue if the student has not received a diploma from his or her high school. It is in the realm of the special education supervisor or director to find these enclaves and job coaches so that the student has realistic expectations of what employment looks and feels like in the private sector.

The supervisor needs to attempt to partner with outside agencies and begin strong communication and alignment with these outside service organizations. The appropriate agencies should always be included in any IEP or evaluation team report (ETR) meetings. Working in unison may detect where there are service gaps for these students between organizations and agencies. Working together also gives the outside agencies an understanding of what skills the student will have in place prior to exiting high school.

Transition plans should also include financial skill instruction and self-help skills such as laundry, cooking, and shopping. Appropriate socialization should be embedded into every lesson. Basic first aid and safety skills with fire, electricity, and stranger danger should also be incorporated into instructional practices. In secondary education, the transition plan is the most important document in the IEP because it will ensure success in years after high school.

Transition plans and their implementation have a long way to go in most school settings. Instructors are not clear and need professional development as to what constitutes a strong measurable transition plan on the IEP. The importance of these plans cannot be stressed enough to faculty. In longevity studies, there is a strong correlation that adults with special education needs such as learning, cognitive, behavior, and emotional disabilities are entering correctional institutions at rates of four to five times more than the general population (Rutherford et al., 2002).

INTEGRATING THEORY INTO PRACTICE

Appropriate transition services for secondary students with special needs are essential to the success of any student and directly affect their long-term quality of life. Too often special education teachers look at only the here and now and how to help the student pass a certain class and do not look long term as to the needs of the adolescent. It is the responsibility of the special education supervisor or director to ensure that a consistent, well-established program is in place for any or all students with IEPs. Developing this system can be difficult because depending upon the needs of the student, each plan should look and be implemented differently. A one-size-fits-all program will not work and will not have successful long-term results.

Usually supervisors or directors have extended time over the summer months to finish out and plan for the next school year. If the district does not have the financial means to appoint someone as a transition coordinator, then the supervisor must get creative to ensure there is a program in place. This creativity involves using the extended time to work with community businesses and hospitals to secure possible placements for the following school year.

Paraprofessionals can become job coaches for these different settings if they are trained on how to coach and not "tell" or "do" for the student. The positions acquired do not have to be paid positions and should rotate to give students different types of work experiences. Vocational inventories need to be purchased so that students can have the opportunity to look at their interests and their abilities while still participating in these different vocational situations.

Recognition for these potential employers should be celebrated annually. The supervisor or director may also want to develop and construct presentations to community organizations like Rotary or local chamber of commerce groups to try to begin to establish contacts for future employment options for the special needs populations.

Students with less severe disabilities need to transition differently by exploring postsecondary options as well as the military. Postsecondary schools should offer both programs and services. Offering a program usually means staff has been hired to assist students to be successful in their university. Services are things like copies of notes, the use of recording devices during classes, and the possibility of extended time on tests and exams.

Transition plans are what should be driving the IEP goals and objectives from the age of fourteen through high school. It is the supervisor's responsibility to ensure that every secondary student has a well-written, data-driven, measurable transition plan with all aspects of the student's disabilities intertwined into the program. Staff members must have professional development, and more than just once a year, if a program is going to be viable and students are going to successful with a strong quality of life.

CASE STUDY

• A parent requests that his or her child graduate with his or her class. After graduation you receive a call from an attorney stating that you did not prepare the child appropriately for adult life. The student just sits at home and watches television. The parent is requesting that the district provide appropriate transition services instead of being sued. How do you respond?

- You would like to assist in the development of a transition program at the high school. You must use existing staff because the levy did not pass. What would your program look like for the students?
- A parent during an IEP meeting does not appear to have realistic goals for his or her child. They expect the student to attend a four-year university. The child is not functioning at that level of performance. How do you assist the parent in recognizing what you feel is more realistic in future planning for the child?

REFERENCES

Hanover Research. (2012). *Supporting Special Education Students in their Transition to Post Secondary Education*. Washington, DC. Retrieved October 11, 2012, from http://www.nlts2.org.

National Longitudinal Transition Study-2. (2005). *After High School: A First Look at the Postschool Experiences of Youth with Disabilities: A Report from the National Longitudinal Transition Study-2 (NLTS2) Prepared for Office of Special Education Programs, U.S. Department of Education*. Menlo Park, CA: SRI International.

Rutherford, R. B., Bullis, M., Anderson, C., & Griller-Clark, H. (2002). Youth with Disabilities in Juvenile Corrections: A National Survey. *Exceptional Children*, Vol. 71, No. 3: 339–345.

Stodden, R. A., & Mruzek, D. W. (2010). An Introduction to Postsecondary Education and Employment of Persons with Autism and Developmental Disabilities. *Focus and Autism and Other Developmental Disabilities,* Vol. 25, No. 3: 131–133.

POINTS TO REMEMBER

- Every child must have a transition plan before their fourteenth birthday.
- The transition plan should drive the individualized educational plan goals and objectives.
- Many adolescents who have developmental disabilities struggle to have something viable to do after graduation.
- The public school system needs to provide opportunities for these adolescents in the community so that appropriate work behaviors can be mastered.

Chapter Eleven

Assistive Technology

THEORY

Every public school system is required to ensure that assistive technology and services are available, if necessary, for any student needing a device to receive a free and appropriate public education (FAPE). An assistive technology device is any item or piece of equipment that has been purchased, modified, created, or customized to improve or increase or just maintain the functional capabilities of a child (Authority: 20 U.S.C. 1401 [1]) IDEA, 04).

There are two components to implementing a successful district assistive technology strategy. The district must attempt to determine the specific needs of the student. Once that assessment is completed then the implementation phase begins. The team needs to attempt using different devices or technologies to ensure whatever system is selected meets the student's needs.

The evaluation component of assistive technology needs to be functional in the student's typical environment. The child should not be isolated for the assessment. The district can lease, borrow, or purchase items to try with the student. Borrowing technology is the most prudent avenue to begin the assessment process to decrease cost for the district.

Every individualized educational plan (IEP) team is required to "consider" a student's need for assistive technology. There are few guidelines in place for a district to implement this service (Reed, 2004). An IEP team must look thoughtfully at assistive technology as a consideration for the student. At least one member of a team should be proficient in implementing technology.

School districts are required to not only discuss technology at an IEP but also discuss what types of services are necessary for the child to be successful. Services may include the evaluation or assessment for the student and training of the student and staff members who are going to be implementing the device. Family members may need training also if the team determines it is appropriate for the student's success.

The reauthorization of the Individuals with Disabilities Education Act (IDEA) of 2004 was put in direct alignment with the No Child Left Behind Act of 2001. This connection examined the necessity to implement alternative text formats or forms for students who had difficulty interacting with traditional text books. This can be interpreted as the need to provide appropriate instructional materials for students who are blind or have a print disability (NIMAS, 2006). A child with dyslexia or fluency difficulties would fit into this category.

Many districts have breezed over the assistive technology services page on the IEP. Districts may not have anyone trained in assistive technology or only have one person in the district who is tech savvy. However, in most cases the tech person may be too busy to assist or attend IEP meetings.

It is important for a district to have a small team responsible for assistive technology. The team should be comprised of a special education administrator, an occupational therapist or physical therapist, a speech and language pathologist, a psychologist, and a classroom teacher who works with children who have disabilities (Reed, 2004).

The special education supervisor or director must ensure that the teachers working with children who have disabilities and teachers of typical children are at least aware of what assistive technology is and what it can do to assist a student in being successful in the classroom. The supervisor must also ensure there is a team available to assess a student if technology is necessary for the student to gain access successfully to the curriculum.

When the IEP team determines that an assessment is necessary for a student, the task that the classroom instructor wants the student to complete needs to be analyzed in detail. This entails asking some specific questions. What is the task with which the student needs assistance to complete? Will the technology limit the need or lessen the need for direct personal assistance? Is the student already able to complete the assignment with special accommodations or strategies? Once these questions are answered, the IEP team should have some direction in the process.

Many times the state department or a county agency may have different technologies available for a team to try with a student before making a formal and final determination. The most important consideration is ensuring the team members communicate with one another during the assessment and implementation process. A child being assessed may not feel well or be coming down with a health issue, and the team may not get a good read on the student and the technology used by the student.

The law requires that the assistive technology component of the services page on the IEP not be glazed over by a team. It is necessary for the director or supervisor to ensure that professional development for staff members addresses this need and that there is a team in place to meet this need.

INTEGRATING THEORY INTO PRACTICE

Many smaller districts have not considered assistive technology during an IEP meeting because there are too many other day-to-day issues that need immediate attention by the supervisor or director. The law is specific, however, so it is essential that the director make this a priority, especially for offering children with print disabilities software to read the text aloud.

The supervisor contacting the technology department within the district is a good way to begin looking at a team formation. The resident tech person can give direction as to what will and what will not work on the district's network system. This contact will prevent purchasing something that the system cannot handle.

Utilizing the occupational therapist and the physical therapist also will help with any types of adaptations necessary to make materials or school-related items accessible to the student. The occupational therapist and the physical therapist spend much of their time outside of therapy creating items to help make things easier for a student to manipulate.

Many districts currently are developing a collaborative with other local districts in the vicinity to cut down on expensive equipment and duplicate expenditures. Developing a central warehouse or library between districts may provide better services for children due to the shared expense of all districts involved within the collaborative.

Assistive technology is a service that is required on an IEP. Training staff members to utilize the same language when discussing items on an IEP will provide consistency in a district and will assist in not getting a district or a school in legal constraints.

CASE STUDIES

- At an IEP meeting a parent advocate requests a specific product for assistive technology for a student. The teacher writes the program into the IEP. When looking at the software purchase, the technology director within the district tells you that that piece of software will not fit on the district network appropriately, and it cannot be purchased. How do you handle this situation with the parent and the advocate, since it is on the signed IEP?
- You are not available to attend an IEP with a contentious parent. You receive a message from an advocate who attended the meeting saying that the teacher skipped over the assistive technology part of the IEP, and

when she was questioned, she said, "We don't do that in this district." How do you address this situation with the parent, the advocate, and the staff member?
- At an IEP meeting a parent requests a certain type of brand name equipment for their child. When you research this equipment you realize that it is an expenditure your department cannot afford. There is another device that does not have all of the bells and whistles but will accomplish the same task for the student. How do you talk the parent into the less expensive technology?

REFERENCES

Golden, D. (1998). *Assistive Technology in Special Education Policy and Practice.* Albuquerque, NM: Council of Administrators of Special Education.
National Center on Accessible Instructional Materials. (2006). Posted by OSEP at the Library of Congress at CAST, Inc.
Reed, P. (2004). *Assessing Students' Needs for Assistive Technology.* Oshkosh, WI: Wisconsin Assistive Technology Initiative.

POINTS TO REMEMBER

- Many school districts ignore assistive technology services that are required to be considered on the IEP service page.
- School districts need to formulate teams to develop technology recommendations for a student.
- The team needs to assess the child's needs and then implement a tool that will assist the child in being successful in school.

Chapter Twelve

Communication

THEORY

Leadership in schools changes on a more rapid basis than it has in the last few decades. Administrators work in numerous districts throughout the country and continually attempt to move up to the next position. Sustaining a strong leadership style of excellence after an administrator leaves can be difficult, and in fact, may cause a vacuum in some districts until the next leader establishes himself or herself with the learning community (Rourke & Hartzman, 2009).

As a supervisor or director for special education it is imperative that a collaborative style of communication is used with the parents, the teachers, and the building administrators. This means everyone must feel like they have a voice and are heard by the leader of the program. The director or supervisor must create a structure that allows for constant feedback and input from all constituents (Rourke & Hartzman, 2009).

Approximately seventy percent of all leaders' time is spent in communication with all stakeholders (Kmetz & Willower, 1982). The role of a leader involves verbal communication, written communication, and communication through actions (Keil & McConnahan, 2005). Communication varies between the sender's and receiver's backgrounds and interpretations of the message being sent. Developing a systems approach to strong communication is the responsibility of the special education director or leader of the program.

Therefore, a strong system and structure of communication is the responsibility of the supervisor or director of the special needs program(s). The communication of word of mouth and networking within a district can make or break a supervisor. Some guidelines to consider when communicating are to write only what the leader can live with being published. In other words, the supervisor must write for the record. Emails are public record and can be requested by anyone in the public.

Only use emails for positives not negatives. Emails can be forwarded, and it is great public relations to have a positive note or a thank you forwarded to other people by the receiver. Lastly, always conduct important conversations in person. This may not always be convenient, but it will bring better outcomes long term (Williams & Riddile, 2012).

Customer service is the name of the game for a supervisor or director of special education. A survey was completed in 2001 asking parents to rate the following communication strategies with school personnel: the number of positive contacts made per year with a family, how quickly a parent is contacted when there is a concern, how frequently parents and school leaders work together, and how often parents feel that their voice is heard by the department leader (Gaunt & Whale, 2001).

It is the special education leader's responsibility, based upon the climate that is within the district, to determine how and when to implement these evidence-based strategies. This implementation structure will ultimately determine the success or failure of the leader of the program.

INTEGRATING THEORY INTO PRACTICE

As a new administrator within a district, the leader must take an appraisal of what has been done in the past and what has been successful and what has failed in terms of communication strategies. This can be done by meeting with all building leaders and the department's supervisor in central office. The director may also want to meet with all of the constituents that report to him or her, such as the psychologists, speech and language pathologists, motor team comprised of occupational therapists and physical therapists, and adaptive physical education instructors.

Meeting with a vocal group of parents who have not been satisfied in the past will also give the director some direction. A strong leader will pull the unsatisfied customers in close proximity so constructive changes in the program may occur. A parent is not as afraid to voice a negative opinion as someone who directly reports to his or her supervisor. A leader will use these negative voices to assist in developing a parent organization that can meet on a regular basis.

The parent group should have a different speaker at each meeting, representing the needs of the different stakeholders of the group. This can be accomplished during the first meeting by asking for topics that parents would like more information about for the continued success of their child in school. Mailings should include the topic, the speaker, and the location and time of each meeting.

The second half of the meeting after the speaker is dismissed should be spent networking with parents and listening to concerns regarding how the needs of their child are not being met to their satisfaction.

This spontaneous parental communication with the leader is a critical time for the program because this is when the parent will determine if the leader walks the talk or through his or her actions can correct the issues and begin to be trusted by the families. The supervisor must be ready for any type of complaint. The concern probably cannot be answered at that meeting; however, the supervisor must get back to the parent in the time frame that he or she establishes with the parent at that meeting.

A veteran supervisor will admit when he or she is unsure of a response to a question but will get back with the parent once he or she accesses the necessary information to answer the question. It is imperative that the supervisor does not get impatient trying to build trust because it was not lost in one encounter and will not return in one encounter but over a long period of time.

Directing a special education program for a district can be a negative experience because most of the emails, phone calls, and communications that the leader receives are based upon problems. The adage "no news is good news" really is true in this position. Constituents of parents, teachers, and building administrators only contact the director when there is a problem or something needs to be done about an issue. Therefore, being able to leave work at work will always assist in the mental health of a supervisor.

The supervisor also needs to determine how he or she gets subtle rewards from the position such as decreasing lawsuits filed, developing programs that are successful, or having parents contact the leader out of trust knowing the supervisor is a problem solver, and his or her interest is advocating for the children.

If a district is struggling, contracting with a university special education program to do an audit of the files and interviews of parents, teachers, and children may give the program some strong direction. Any findings will be public record, however, and the leader must be in a position to work through the weaknesses of the program that are noted.

Another way to get customer feedback is to construct a survey of parents, teachers, and building leaders to get the flavor of the strengths and weaknesses in a program. These results should also be shared publicly so that the program is transparent and can grow from the critique with the support of the stakeholders.

Lastly, it is imperative from all of this constructive feedback that the program develops a shared vision to communicate the nature and culture of the new program. Through this type of collaboration a program will have integrity and will have recognizable goals and objectives. Once these are established, then all the director must do is to manage and facilitate this vision to ensure that all children receive the best education available to them on his or her watch.

CASE STUDIES

- During an initial parent club meeting that you started and facilitate monthly, a parent complains vehemently about a teacher and his or her educational practices. The teacher is sitting in the audience and gets very offended and walks out. Even though you try to deflect the conversation the damage is done. You receive a call the next day from your supervisor who is very angry at the outcome. How do you handle this situation?
- A parent contacts you about a problem he or she is having in the schools. You listen attentively and attempt to console the parent. The parent interprets that empathy as you are agreeing with the parent's point of view. He or she marches into the school the next day and confronts the principal and the teacher about your agreement with how the school is handling her child. You never had time to warn the school personnel because of another crisis. What is your response now that a trust level could be broken with either the school or the parent?
- A parent misunderstands you when you tell him that he or she can bring an advocate. At the meeting, the advocate presents an invoice expecting payment from the school based upon your recommendation of his or attendance at the meeting. It was not your intent to portray a recommendation like that to the parent. Who pays for the service?

REFERENCES

Gaunt, M. A., & Whale, D. E. (2001). Customer Service: Are We Doing as Well as We Think? *Principal Leadership*, Vol. 2, No. 1: 40–41.

Keil, V. L., & McConnahan, W. R. (2005). Meaningful Written Communication by Administrators. *Connections,* Vol. 7: 20–26.

Kmetz, J. T., & Willower, D. J. (1982). Elementary School Principals' Work Behavior. *Educational Administrator Quarterly,* Vol. 4: 62–68.

Reyes, P., & Hoyle, D. (1992). Teachers' Satisfaction with Principals' Communication. *Journal of Educational Research,* Vol. 85: 163–168.

Rourke, J., & Hartzman, M. (2009). Giano Middle School: The Parent Factor. *Principal Leadership,* Vol. 9, No. 10: 24–27.

Williams, J., & Riddile, M. (2012). The Principal Difference Blog, National Association of Secondary School Principals. Retrieved October 15, 2012 from, www.nassp.org/tabid/3788/default.aspx.

POINTS TO REMEMBER

- It is imperative that a collaborative style of communication is implemented by every director.
- Seventy percent of a director's time is spent in communication with all stakeholders.
- Starting a parent group for parents of children with special needs allows parents to network and be educated on the law and on different services allowed by law; a parent group also provides a method for parents to network with one another and the director or supervisor.

Chapter Thirteen

Leadership

THEORY

It is the responsibility of a director or supervisor to ensure all adults within the system are committed and dedicated to building community within a school district. As the adults within the district model this behavior, the families and children attending the schools will also become assimilated to that belonging feeling. Students in caring communities will achieve higher results scholastically and develop a stronger social development ethic within a school setting because of that nurturing (Schaps & Solomon, 1990).

Parents need the support of a strong listening supervisor as they grieve over and adapt to the disabilities of their child. With that grief will develop anger if the school system is not following through on what they promised through the individualized educational plan (IEP) or 504 plan, and if the child is not making the growth on his or her goals that were promised during the meeting. A strong leader can manage a department or a program while instilling and weaving the necessary ethical values of honesty and compassion with families into the daily standards-based academic pedagogy (Starratt, 1991).

This compassion will produce resiliency within families. Resilient people can face difficult situations without overreacting, giving up, or resorting to anger (Edwards, 2000). In simpler terms, resiliency means there is a strong positive outcome for a family that has experienced a major risk factor or trauma (Brooks, 1998). Having a child with a disability can be earth shattering to many families. Many researchers have connected resiliency with schools, with families, and with children being directly related to administrators building healthy, productive, caring relationships with these parents (Paredes, 1993).

The vulnerability and stress of sitting in a large group of strangers discussing the weaknesses and strengths of a child can be devastating and can dramatically affect future positive relationships between the school and the family (Swanson & Schneider, 1999). It is the administrator's responsibility to create an atmosphere or climate that welcomes all families and children to the learning community and creates a culture that is caring and connected (Sergiovanni, 1992).

It is the supervisor or director's responsibility to create and maintain this caring community climate in the IEP or 504 meetings, in the communication systems, and when problems or issues arise (Edwards, 2000). If trust is established from the beginning, teams of parents and professionals can problem solve together for the well-being and resiliency of the child.

Many times as a leader builds trust with his or her customers and employees, there is a feeling of pronounced isolation as a director or supervisor making management decisions. There is not always someone to brainstorm with or communicate how difficult certain situations may be becoming for the isolated manager. Many times leaders will be strongly motivated, regardless of the work they perform, if there is a sense of affiliation with an organization, a sense of trust, and a feeling of being personally valued by their constituents (Fukuyama, 1995).

This sense of personal trust must be derived from a social context in which many virtues, such as honesty, reliability, and cooperation, are present within the top of an organization (Fouche, 2006). These values will assist the leader in becoming more engaged with the organization and reduce the isolation of making decisions for employees or students without possible interaction with peers or immediate supervisors. When leaders put trust in other colleagues of similar position or ranking, the feelings of isolation are reduced because this interaction creates a common set of norms, retention of supervisors is stronger, there is greater productivity for all employees and students, and parent satisfaction will increase dramatically (Fouche, 2006).

Therefore, it is critical for organizations to gain greater insight into the isolation administrators may feel and encourage common discussions with colleagues regarding the district norms and values, encouragement from leaders, and positive reinforcement from superintendents for the work that is being done on behalf of the students (Dolan, 2011). Creating a professional learning community between like positions may encourage the trust and the conversation between leaders. These social connections with like positioned coworkers have been noted to be a strong predictor of job satisfaction and thus retention of strong leaders and employees (Putnam, 2000).

It is not uncommon for supervisors to feel frustrated, out of touch, and isolated without frequent interactions with coworkers of like position. This interaction encourages discussions of common problems and allows the supervisor or director a safe place to vent with another person of equal position who can understand the problems and dilemmas. By providing this venue for discussion and concerns within the supervisory organization, workers tend to be more inclined to participate and volunteer in work-related after-hour activities and local civic responsibilities (Edwards & Shepherd, 2007).

INTEGRATING THEORY INTO PRACTICE

There are two types of isolation that both the parent and the supervisor may experience in school settings. When parents learn that their pride and joy, the child of their dreams, has something not quite right happening in the school setting, a feeling of denial, blame, and grieving occurs on the parental side. The parents need to have the time to work through this critical, difficult time in their family. Usually the parents discover these concerns in a meeting of multiple strangers and professionals.

The parents come into this frightening meeting hoping to leave with clarification and a treatment or prescription to fix the concerns for their child. What they hear are strangers spending the bulk of the meeting discussing the issues and the problems of what is wrong with their child, almost as if they are admiring the problem, rather than spending their efforts trying to strategize solutions and accommodations to assist the child in being successful.

These meetings may be multistep meetings where the team discusses ways to intervene, and then sets time lines on how the team will respond to these interventions. Unfortunately, the explanation of the actual meeting process is not always delineated to the parent, so it just appears as if negatives about their child are continually discussed without resolution or a prescription to address the concerns. This creates anger and resentment on behalf of the parents, and they begin to shut down.

It is the responsibility of a supervisor or director to educate the parents prior to participating in this type of meeting. Special education parents and 504 parents need an outlet where they can network and connect with parents who have experienced the same situation and have a common value and concern. The director needs to create this venue by beginning a parent group that will allow these concerns to be voiced and heard by central office administration.

A special education supervisor or director can invite parents monthly or every other month to an evening meeting where the focus can be education for the parents of current changes in education, as well as a time at the end of the meeting to voice concerns and complaints to the leader of special education, gifted and talented, or English as a second language.

The leader must take notes and problem solve some of those concerns shared by the parents by getting back to those parents who have questions, concerns, or misunderstandings. The leader does not have to respond that night, but must follow through within a period of days to begin or maintain a trust level with these parents so that they feel they have been heard. This give-and-take interaction will build trust, as well as give the director or supervisor a sense of the pulse of the district based upon the complaints and concerns given by the customers.

The concerns the leader discovers gives room to determine where professional development is needed and what additional education is necessary so that the parents begin to understand how to navigate the maze of special education. If the leader is new in the situation, a survey or an audit might be arranged to glean more information about the needs of the district as well as the major concerns that are currently brewing in the community. The data obtained from this type of research will allow a leader to set goals and objectives and plot out the direction that the department should try to follow together.

When the report of the survey or the audit becomes public, the director should form a committee comprised of parents, teachers, principals, psychologists, speech and language pathologists, occupational therapists, and physical therapists. This group can then take the weaknesses and turn them into measurable action plans to change the focus of the department, which will ultimately impact the school system positively. Having all constituents involved in the process begins to build trust and ownership of the issues so that unbiased solutions can be discussed and realized by the group.

The presentation of this action plan should be given by all members of the committee that developed the strategic action plan with measurable dates for the outcome, and data as evidence of the accomplishments of the group. During this presentation, the leader should take a back seat so that the constituents have more ownership, which will lead to success and trust being built within the district.

As a supervisor, the isolation as a leader is a real concern. Everyone needs a sounding board, and the director or supervisor needs to find someone within the organization to vent and problem solve with who will not talk out of turn but listen and assist in the development of solutions. Finding someone within the organization will be of greater value to the leader rather than someone outside of the organization. Those employees within the system have an understanding of the dynamics and complications that are ever present within the community.

Once the leader has located a person of similar position with whom to share concerns and problems, a professional friendship will develop within the job, and common values and norms will be established within the new-found friendship. This will assist in the position and responsibilities not seeming as difficult, and the leader will not feel so alone and isolated. This helps build self-esteem, retention, and loyalty to the organization.

Being a leader is a lonely job but very fulfilling if the director or supervisor keeps the focus on the students and their individual needs and successes. With that common denominator, the special education, gifted, or English as a second language department will stay centered on doing what is right for children, and the outcome will be beneficial to all.

CASE STUDIES

- You accept a new position as a supervisor, and there does not appear to be any trust in the system. What are some things you can you do to attempt to bring back this attribute?
- You have instructed the intervention specialists to write thorough curriculum-based-data-driven IEPs. You have given them examples and brought in speakers, but the staff still is not writing measurable objectives. What is your next response?
- The district does not believe in the concept of inclusion for most children on IEPs. Most of the students are either self-contained or receiving subpar instruction in the resource classroom. The intervention specialists are working diligently to provide appropriate instruction, yet they do not have access to the core or the materials necessary to try to implement a modified core. Parents are concerned that their children are not getting free and appropriate public education. The typical teachers that do co-teach change annually so they do not have to have children with special needs in their classroom annually. The typical classrooms have about fifty percent IEP students and fifteen percent 504 students in each section, so it really does not look like an inclusion class. Where do you begin to try and change the culture and the services?

REFERENCES

Brooks, R. (1998). To Foster Children's Self-Esteem and Resilience, Search for Islands of Competence. *The Brown University Child and Adolescent Behavior Letter*, Vol. 14, No. 6.

Dolan, V. (2011). The Isolation of Online Adjunct Faculty and Its Impact on their Performance. *International Review of Research in Open and Distance Learning*, Vol. 12, No. 2: 63–77.

Edwards, A. P., & Shepherd, G. J. (2007). An Investigation of the Relationship between Implicit Personal Theories of Communication and Community Behavior. *Communication Studies*, Vol. 58, No. 4: 359–375.

Edwards, C. (2000). Moral Classroom Communities and the Development of Resiliency. *Contemporary Education*, Vol. 71, No. 4: 1–5.

Fouche, I. (2006). A Multi-island Situation without the Ocean: Tutors' Perceptions about Working in Isolation from Colleagues. *International Review of Research in Open and Distance Learning*, Vol. 7, No. 2. Retrieved December 17, 2012, from http://www.irrodl.org/index.php/irrodl/article/view/295/640.

Fukuyama, F. (1995). *Trust: The Social Virtues and the Creation of Prosperity*. New York: Free Press.

Paredes, V. (1993 April). School Correlates with Student Persistence to Stay in School. Paper presented at the annual meeting of the American Educational Research Association, Atlanta. ERIC Document Reproduction Service No. ED 359 599.

Putnam, R. D. (2000). *Bowling Alone: The Collapse and Revival of American Community*, 1st ed. New York: Simon & Schuster.

Schaps, E., & Solomon, D. (1990). Schools and Classrooms as Caring Communities. *Educational Administration Quarterly*, Vol. 27, No. 2: 185–202.

Sergiovanni, T. (1992). *Moral Leadership: Getting to the Heart of School Improvement*. San Francisco: Jossey-Bass.

Starratt, R. (1991). Building an Ethical School: A Theory for Practice in Educational Leadership. *Educational Administration Quarterly*, Vol. 27, No. 2: 185–202.

Swanson, C., & Schneider, B. (1999). Students on the Move: Residential and Educational Mobility in American Schools. *Sociology of Education*, Vol. 72, No. 1: 54–67.

POINTS TO REMEMBER

- A new director or supervisor must establish themselves as a credible coordinator and facilitator.
- Being a supervisor can create a very isolated feeling for the individual in this position.
- It is the responsibility of a strong leader to listen more than talk and model the changes that he or she wants to implement.
- A supervisor or leader needs to find a strong sounding board for his or her issues, problems, or solutions. Without this feedback, the leader can make errors in judgment, and the turnover in the position can be very high.

Epilogue

CHAPTER 1: INTERVENTION

- All school systems must implement a universal screener to assess who is falling behind grade level. New enrollees should also be screened so that they can be placed in the appropriate section or class.
- Benchmarking is a means of collecting a baseline on a student. Progress monitoring should be completed at set intervals throughout the school year.
- Special education needs to be a service not a place where children receive intervention.

CHAPTER 2: THE LAWS

- The Individuals with Disabilities Education Act was authorized to provide a free and appropriate public education for all children.
- The law also addresses intervention as something that utilizes evidence-based strategies that will make a significant positive difference in the life of a child.
- Section 504 of the Rehabilitation Act of 1973 describes the section that a person with a medical impairment cannot be discriminated against. This is the rationale for a 504 plan.
- Prior to a multifactored evaluation, a school team must intervene, look at the data, and respond appropriately to that data and make decisions. This is called Response to Intervention.
- Individualized educational plans can generate federal funding; however, 504 plans are a general education initiative and the cost is picked up by the school district.

CHAPTER 3: AUTISM

- If you have seen one child with autism you have seen one child with autism. Children who have autism present very differently from one another.
- Children with autism do respond better with visuals and evidence-based treatment programs.
- Applied behavior analysis is a systematic treatment program, which is one of the only programs that has evidence that it does make a positive difference in children with autism.
- Children with autism perform better with appropriate peer models. Video modeling also has proven to make a positive difference with children with autism.
- Sensory input can assist a student in self-regulation.
- Autism is a medical diagnosis. Just because a student has the label of having autism does not mean that he or she immediately needs an IEP or 504 plan. Those should only be implemented if the autism is having an adverse effect of either academics or social interaction with peers.

CHAPTER 4: GIFTED AND TALENTED

- Response to Intervention should also be used in gifted identification.
- Children who have been identified as being gifted must have appropriate intervention and services or their IQ will fall back toward the mean score.
- Children identified as being gifted need the rigor of instruction increased with integration of critical thinking skills.
- Gifted instructors can instruct using a pull-out program or co-teaching with the classroom teacher.
- Acceleration by subject or grade level is a means to instruct gifted children. A protocol that is evidence based should be utilized to assist with the team decision on whether to accelerate or not accelerate a child.
- Differentiation is a means to meet the needs of all children within a classroom.
- A written education plan should be developed for children who are identified as gifted and talented. A written acceleration plan should be developed for children who may be subject- or grade-level accelerated. All plans should be reviewed at least annually or if there is a concern.

CHAPTER 5: THE TWICE-EXCEPTIONAL CHILD

- Children can be identified as having a disability, as well as being identified as gifted and talented.
- It is essential that children who are twice exceptional receive intervention for both their giftedness and their disability. This can be a challenge to intervene for staff members.
- Many gifted children and twice-exceptional children struggle with social skills. This deficit needs to be addressed to ensure a child is successful in all endeavors.

CHAPTER 6: ENGLISH AS A SECOND LANGUAGE

- English as a second language is also referred to as limited English proficiency.
- All school districts must have a plan to service these children as it is a federal mandate.
- Section 601 of the Civil Rights Act of 1964 prohibits discrimination on the basis of race, color, or natural origin. The LEP program falls under this determination.
- When a child is initially enrolled in a district, a language survey should be completed by the parent to determine if a student needs LEP services.
- There are varied service delivery models from tutoring to pull out to actual classrooms that are bilingual.
- English is assessed annually and children cannot be dismissed by a district until they score above the fluent and proficient levels.

CHAPTER 7: DYSLEXIA

- "Dyslexia is a specific learning disability that is neurobiological in origin. It is characterized by difficulties with accurate and/or fluent word recognition and by poor spelling and decoding abilities. These difficulties typically result from a deficit in the phonological component of language that is often unexpected in relation to other cognitive abilities and the provision of effective classroom instruction" (International Dyslexia Association as cited in Shaywitz, 2003).
- Treatment for dyslexia needs to be a systematic, multisensory, evidence-based program.
- Magnetic resonance imaging (MRI) tests have been completed and children who have had the correct treatment for dyslexia show a medical difference before and after the multisensory, scripted, evidence-based strategy and intervention.

CHAPTER 8: DEVELOPMENTAL DELAYS

- Section 504 of the Rehabilitation Act of 1973 prohibited federal funding for school systems that discriminated against children who had developmental delays.
- Children need to be included as much as possible in the typical classroom so that they are exposed to the core content.
- Standards-based individualized educational plans need to be written so that children who have developmental delays can access the Common Core curriculum.

CHAPTER 9: EMOTIONAL DISTURBANCE

- Children with an emotional disturbance must display behaviors over a long period of time, to a marked degree, and these behaviors must have an adverse reaction on the child in question.
- A child who is socially maladjusted or has been traumatically impacted by divorce or death cannot qualify for these services.
- The classroom environment and the behavior plan should have a positive impact on the child's behavior. A functional behavior assessment must be completed prior to developing a behavior plan for a child.

CHAPTER 10: TRANSITION

- Every child must have a transition plan before their fourteenth birthday.
- The transition plan should drive the individualized educational plan goals and objectives.
- Many adolescents who have developmental disabilities struggle to have something viable to do after graduation.
- The public school system needs to provide opportunities for these adolescents in the community so that appropriate work behaviors can be mastered.

CHAPTER 11: ASSISTIVE TECHNOLOGY

- Many school districts ignore assistive technology services that are required to be considered on the IEP service page.
- School districts need to formulate teams to develop technology recommendations for a student.
- The team needs to assess the child's needs and then implement a tool that will assist the child in being successful in school.

CHAPTER 12: COMMUNICATION

- It is imperative that a collaborative style of communication is implemented by every director.
- Seventy percent of a director's time is spent in communication with all stakeholders.
- Starting a parent group for parents of children with special needs allows parents to network and be educated on the law; a parent group also provides a method for parents to network with one another and the director or supervisor.

CHAPTER 13: LEADERSHIP

- A new director or supervisor must establish themselves as a credible coordinator and facilitator.
- Being a supervisor can create a very isolated feeling for the individual in this position.
- It is the responsibility of a strong leader to listen more than talk and model the changes that he or she wants to implement.
- A supervisor or leader needs to find a strong sounding board for his or her issues, problems, or solutions. Without this feedback, the leader can make errors in judgment, and the turnover in the position can be very high.

About the Author

Kevin A. Gorman has been in education for more than thirty-six years. He has been principal of a high school and an alternate school, director of pupil services, director of intervention, and a classroom teacher. He has taught both undergraduate- and masters-level college courses in the field of education. This is his second education book.